Marek J. Murawski

Focke-Wulf Ta 152

KAGERO

MORE FROM KAGERO

www.shop.kagero.pl • phone + 4881 5012105

Focke-Wulf Ta 152 • Marek J. Murawski • First edition • LUBLIN 2016

© All rights reserved. With the exception of quoting brief passages for the purposes of review, no part of this publication may be reproduced without prior written permission from the Publisher. Nazwa serii zastrzeżona w UP RP • ISBN 978-83-64596-93-3

Editing: **Marek J. Murawski** • Translation: **Piotr Kolasa** • Cover artwork: **Antonis Karidis** • Color profiles: **Arkadiusz Wróbel** • Drawings: **Stefan Dramiński** • Photos: **Marek J. Murawski's archive, Kagero's archive** • Design: **KAGERO STUDIO, Marcin Wachowicz**

Oficyna Wydawnicza KAGERO
Akacjowa 100, Turka, os. Borek, 20-258 Lublin 62, Poland, phone/fax: (+48) 81 501 21 05
www.kagero.pl • e-mail: kagero@kagero.pl, marketing@kagero.pl
w w w . k a g e r o . p l
Distribution: **Oficyna Wydawnicza KAGERO**

Focke-Wulf Fw 190 A-3/U7, W.Nr. 0528 was one of the first three experimental aircraft used in the development of the high-altitude fighter program.

Introduction

The events of World War 2 proved beyond any doubt that the strategic bombing campaign greatly contributed to the Allies' ultimate victory over Nazi Germany. British night bombing raids and daylight carpet bombing missions flown by the USAAF crews rained destruction on German cities killing thousands of civilians in the process. Amidst this massive loss of civilian life the destruction of German industrial targets seemed almost like a side note. The arms race that kicked off even before the war began produced military aircraft capable of reaching ever higher operational ceilings. At first thin air at high altitudes was the domain of reconnaissance machines, but before long fighter and bomber aircraft began to venture there as well. In those early days high-altitude flight was a challenging business: it required the use of pressurized cockpits and boosted powerplants capable of delivering adequate power at altitude.

The two most common piston-powered fighter types operated by the Luftwaffe during the war were Messerschmitt Bf 109 and Focke-Wulf Fw 190. The latter, thanks to its sturdy design, proved to be easier to adapt to a variety of roles. It was used as a pure fighter, bomber destroyer, ground attack platform, reconnaissance aircraft and a fighter-bomber. The Fw 190's excellent flight characteristics and a huge development potential inherent to the aircraft's design led to the development of a new high-altitude fighter capable of holding its own against the USAAF escort fighters and heavy bombers.

Powered by a fourteen-cylinder BMW 801 radial engine the standard Focke-Wulf Fw 190 A went into action in mid 1941 and quickly demonstrated its superiority over the RAF's Supermarine Spitfire Mk. V. However, it became clear just as quickly that the BMW 801's stellar performance was limited to altitudes of about 6 000 meters. Aware of his aircraft shortcomings, prof. Kurt Tank, the Fw 190's chief designer, began to look for feasible ways of turning the machine into a true high-altitude fighter. His first step was to take a closer look at the liquid-cooled Daimler-Benz DB 603 A in-line engine. However, the use of the powerplant by Focke-Wulf had to be authorized by the RLM and than there was a daunting task of adapting the Fw 190 airframe to the new engine.

Until those issues could be resolved the Focke-Wulf design team focused on improving high-altitude characteristics of the existing Fw 190 design equipped with the original BMW 801 powerplant. The work had to be done quickly and efficiently since the competition was already busy at work developing their own high-altitude fighter design – the Messerschmitt Bf 109 H.

In mid 1942 the United States entered the war and soon the skies over Europe saw high-flying USAAF heavy bombers. While Bf 109s, equipped with their liquid-cooled Daimler-Benz DB 601 engines, had little trouble operating above 6 000 meters, the Fw 190 was unable to fight at such heights. An interim solution was to be the introduction of light-weight Fw 190 variants: A-4/U5, A-4/U6 and A-4/U7. The Fw 190 A-4/U5's engine was supposed to be moved forward, while most of the aircraft's armor was to be removed. Only the pilot's seat and the area around frame 5 would retain their original armor plating. All armor protection around

Introduction

Fw 190 A-3/U 7 was powered by a radial BMW 801 D engine.

the oil cooler and fuel tanks was stripped. The A-4/U6 variant was even more radical: the only armor left was light protection behind the pilot's seat. The position of the engine mount remained unchanged. The A-4/U7 version was do be identical to the U6 variant with the exception of armor plates protecting the aircraft's oil cooler and fuel tanks. Initially three prototypes of each variant were to be built, but the project was abandoned just a month later in favor of a new design – the Fw 190 A-3/U7. The aircraft was essentially an Fw 190 A-3 airframe partially

Three additional air scoops clearly seen in this head-on shot were designed to improve the airflow into the BMW 801 D at high altitudes.

Fw 190 A-3/U7, W.Nr. 0528 wore a standard Luftwaffe camouflage scheme consisting of patches of RLM 74 Graugrün and RLM 75 Grauviolett on upper surfaces and RLM 76 Lichtblau covering lower wing surfaces and fuselage sides, as well as the vertical fin. The side and lower surfaces were additionally oversprayed with mottles of RLM 02 Grau, RLM 74 Graugrün and RLM 75 Grauviolett. The lower part of the engine cowl was painted yellow.

stripped of armor plating and fuel tank protection, which reduced the fighter's empty weight from 3 850 kg to 3 660 kg. Cockpit armor (including the pilot's seat side and back protection) was removed, but the 48 kg engine armor and the 16 kg bullet-proof windshield remained in place. To further reduce the fighter's weight the design team opted to remove the pair of fuselage-mounted MG 17s, which reduced offensive armament to two wing-mounted MG 151 20 mm cannons. Two air scoops added on each side of the engine bay were designed to improve the BMW 801's high-altitude performance. Further modifications included the replacement of the FuG VII radio with the FuG 16 unit. The FuG 25 set was also removed. The revamped fighter's operational ceiling increased to 12 000 m (previously 11 800 m), while its turn radius at 10 000 m dropped from 1 450 m to 1 250 m.

Three prototypes of the Fw 190 A3/U7 were built in September 1942 (W.Nr. 528, 531 and 532). However, after a series of tests the plans for serial production were abandoned. The main issues proved to be the lack of pressurized cockpit and a rather modest gain in performance at a cost of drastic reduction of offensive armament and decreased pilot protection.

The Focke-Wulf engineers moved on to the next stage – the development of Höhenjäger 1 and Höhenjäger 2 (high-altitude fighter 1 and 2).

Höhenjäger 1 and 2

Höhenjäger 1 was another variant of the Fw 190 featuring a modified BMW 801 D powerplant and the GM-1 nitrous oxide boost system, which allowed the engine power output to increase by as much as 300 HP over a period of up to 15 minutes. The GM-1 installation weighed in at 150 kg. The aircraft was to be equipped with a pressurized cockpit and feature larger wing area (20.3 sq m compared to 18.3 sq m on the standard Fw 190).

The RLM showed considerable interest in the new design and authorized Focke-Wulf to continue work on the project, which was tentatively scheduled to enter serial production in June 1942 as the Fw 190 B-1. In company documents the project was referred to as the Fw 190 Ra-3. The production machines were assigned block numbers starting from W.Nr. 190.0210. The plans called for the production of 2 991 fighters, including 998 assembled at the Focke-Wulf plant, 608 delivered by Fiseler, 685 manufactured by Ago and 700 built by Arado. Production machines were to be armed with two fuselage-mounted 7.92 mm MG 17 guns and four wing-mounted 20 mm cannons (two pairs of 151/20 and MG FF weapons). The avionics suite was to consist of FuG 16 and FuG 25 sets. The aircraft could carry an additional 300 l drop tank on the centerline station.

In the meantime, for reasons unknown, the officials at the RLM had a change of heart and cancelled the original order. Now only six examples of the Fw 190 B-1 were to be built (W.Nr. 811-816). Eventually five of the aircraft (W.Nr. 812-816) were used as test beds in weapons trials of the Fw 190 A-5.

The prototype of the B model was Fw 190 V12, W.Nr. 0035, which was built using the airframe of the last pre-production Fw 190 A-0 variant equipped with pressurized cockpit and the GM-1 boost installation. The airframe was used only very briefly before being scrapped. It was followed by other experimental aircraft,

Höhenjäger 1 and 2

Focke-Wulf Fw 190 A-3/U7, W.Nr. 0531 modified for high-altitude trials. Compared to a standard Fw 190 A-3 weighing 3 850 kg this airframe's weight was reduced to 3 660 kg. The "diet" included the removal of cockpit armor and nose mounted MG 17 7.92 mm machine guns.

first of which was the Fw 190 B-0, W.Nr. 0046, TI+IK. The machine first flew on January 20, 1943 with Werner Bartsch at the controls. Originally the fighter featured pressurized cockpit and the new, larger wing. However, the latter was quickly replaced with the standard 18.3 sq m unit. The fighter had undergone a series of tests at Focke-Wulf before being handed over to Erprobungsstelle Rechlin on June 1, 1943.

Another experimental vehicle was the Fw 190 B-0, W.Nr. 0047, TI+IL, which was first flown by Hans Sander on March 30, 1943. Initially the aircraft was equipped with a single-layer canopy, which proved to be a disappointment in high-altitude operations due to excessive icing. The canopy was soon replaced with a double-layer type, which took care of the icing problem. However, the canopy was still prone to internal fogging, which greatly reduced visibility from the cockpit. The designers experimented with the use of special hygroscopic foil to address the issue. Like its predecessor, the fighter was eventually handed over to E-Stelle Rechlin on January 4, 1944.

The Fw 190 B-0, W.Nr. 0048, TI+IM was the third experimental aircraft. On April 6, 1943 Hans Sander took the fighter for its maiden flight. The machine, similarly to W.Nr. 0047, carried two fuselage-mounted MG 17s and a pair of MG 151/20 cannons mounted in the wing roots. Just like its predecessor, the aircraft featured a standard Fw 190 wing, but was equipped with an upgraded version of the pressurized cockpit. On August 5, 1944 the fighter was slightly damaged (about 10%) during a heavy air raid on Langenhagen factory.

The other two experimental aircraft that followed received production designations Fw 190 B-1. Both machines were powered by the BMW 801 D engines featuring GM-1 boost systems. The first aircraft (Fw 190 B-1, W.Nr. 0049) made its maiden flight on January 11, 1944 when it was ferried from Adelheide to Langenhagen. On February 16, 1944 the fighter was damaged dur-

The same aircraft viewed from behind. Breech covers of two MG 151/20 20 mm cannons can be seen on the wings near the fuselage. The cannons were the only armament the aircraft carried.

ing a forced landing resulting from engine fire. It was quickly repaired and rejoined the test program. On March 23, 1944 the machine was handed over to BMW for further trials.

The second Fw 190 B-1 (W.Nr. 0811, BH+CA) first flew on August 25, 1943. On March 30, 1944 it was ferried to E-Stelle Rechlin, but by that time the GM-1 system had already been removed from the airframe. In its place an additional 115 l fuel tank had been installed.

The last experimental versions of the Fw 190 B were Fw 190 V45 and V 47. Both aircraft were powered by the BMW 801 D-2 engines and featured GM-1 boost systems with a supply of nitrous oxide sufficient for 20 minutes of continuous use. Neither machine had a pressurized cockpit. The Fw 190 V45, RP+IU made its first flight on July 9, 1943 under the designation of Fw 190 A-6/R4. It was then handed over to Rechlin on September 18, 1943 before being ferried to a flying school at Altenburg on October 27, 1944. The Fw 190 V47 was not assembled until February 1944 and it went on to become the experimental airframe for the GM-1 equipped Fw 190 A-8.

While trials of the radial-powered Fw 190 B continued, Tank's team were looking at ways of mating the inline Daimler-Benz DB 603 engine to their design. The re-engined fighter received a temporary designation Höhenjäger 2.

Daimler-Benz engineers began their work on the DB 603 as early as September 1936. However, the RLM's priorities where elsewhere at that time, so the development work was suspended and did not resume until late 1939 and early 1940. In the summer of 1942, during one of the many meetings held to discuss progress of the Fw 190 and Me 309 programs, a decision was made that both types should be ultimately powered by the DB 603. The first Focke-Wulf to receive the DB 603 A-0 powerplant was the Fw 190, W.Nr. 0036, SK+JS. The DB 603 A-0 had a capacity of 4 450 ccm and was capable of delivering dash power output of 1 750 HP at 2 700 rpm. In continuous operation at 5 700 m the engine was rated at 1 375 HP at 2 300 rpm. The powerplant was fully compatible with the GM 1 boost system. The test program using prototypes of the Focke-Wulf Fw 190 C powered by the DB 603 engine eventually led to the full-scale production of the Fw 190 D.

Development of the Ta 152 design

In May 1943 representatives of Focke-Wulf submitted to the RLM's Technical Department (*Technisches Amt*) a proposal to develop a new fighter based on the existing Fw 190 design. Since the proposed aircraft differed significantly from the basic Fw 190, it received the Ta 152 designation on August 17, 1943 – in honor of its chief designer, Kurt Tank.

The Ta 152 project was Focke-Wulf's response to the requirements issued by the Technical Department for a "special fighter" (*Spezial Jäger*) capable of high-altitude operations. The requirements also specified that the new design should be powered by an inline engine (Junkers Jumo 213 E or Daimler-Benz DB 603 E, G or L). In order to save time and avoid radical changes in the design, Kurt Tank opted to equip the new aircraft with an annular engine coolant and oil radiator, which from the outside looked very similar to a radial engine fairing. Originally Tank's design team worked on two variants of the new machine: a standard fighter version designated Ta 152 Ra 1 (Ta 152 V1) and a high-altitude fighter (Ta 152 Ra 2). Shortly after the program had been launched the work on two

The high-altitude variant Fw 190 A-3/U7 never entered mass production. The aircraft's performance was not much different from a standard A-3 model: operating ceiling was 12 000 m compared to A-3's 11 800 m; turning radius at 10 000 m was also only marginally smaller (1 250 m) than A-3's 1 450 m.

Development of the Ta 152 design

Focke-Wulf Fw 190 B-0, W.Nr. 0046, TI+IK made the first flight on January 20, 1943 (pilot: Werner Bartsch). The aircraft featured larger wing with the area of 20,3 m.

A mock-up of the "Einfach-Haube" pressurized cockpit used in the Fw 190 B-0.

more variants began: the Ta 152 Ra 3 ground attack aircraft and the Ta 152 Ra 4 escort fighter.

In the meantime the RLM published their own specifications for the Ta 152. The aircraft was to be powered by a Junkers Jumo 213 A engine mounted in a slightly modified Fw 190 A airframe. The extent of the modifications was to allow future installation of either Jumo 213 E or Daimler-Benz DB 603 G powerplants. The offensive armament was to consist of an engine-mounted MK 103 or MK 108 30 mm cannon. The aircraft powered by the Junkers Jumo 213 A were tentatively designated Ta 152 A, while the model equipped with the Junkers Jumo 213 E powerplant was supposed to become the Ta 152 B. Since at that time the Jumo 213 A could not accommodate the cannon installation, they needed to be replaced with Jumo 213 C models.

In order to allow the installation of the MK 103 30 mm cannon plus a pair of MG 152/20 20 mm weapons, the nose of the aircraft had to be extended by 0.772 m. The nose extension changed the fighter's CG, so the wing attachment points had to be moved forward by 0.420 m. Additionally, a 0.5 m plug was inserted in the rear section of the fuselage to maintain the airframe balance. The additional space was used for pilot's oxygen bottles and compressed air tanks for operation of the cannon. Longer fuselage required stronger structural members. Therefore, aluminum longerons had to be replaced with steel units. The aircraft received a larger vertical stabilizer (1.77 sq m), while the horizontal stabilizers were unmodified Fw 190 assemblies.

Unlike the Fw 190 A with electrically operated landing gear, the Ta 152 A was to be equipped with a hydraulic gear extension and retraction system. The new aircraft would also be heavier than the Fw 190 A, which required the use of larger diameter (740 mm x 210 mm) main wheels.

With larger main wheels installed the main landing gear assemblies had to be moved outboard by 0.250 m, which was possible because the fighter's wingspan was increased from 10.5 m to 11.0 m. The new machine had a completely redesigned wing to fuselage assembly and strengthened wing skin panels to account for the increase in weight.

The aircraft also received brand new flame dampers, since there were plans to use it in a night fighter role operating as part of the *Wilde Sau* system. Later on, after the *Wilde Sau* single-engine fighter units had been withdrawn from operations on April 18, 1944, the flame dampers assemblies on Ta 152s were discarded.

The forward 233 l fuselage fuel tank was an unmodified unit used in the Fw 190 A, although it was mounted slightly more forward because of the changes to the fuselage structure. This arrangement made room for a larg-

Development of the Ta 152 design

er aft fuel tank, whose capacity increased to 362 l. Both fuel tanks received armor protection (16 mm plating on the sides and bottom and 12 mm armor on the top). The aircraft would be able to carry additional 300 l of fuel in a jettisonable drop tank mounted on the centerline hardpoint.

To improve the Ta 152's high-altitude performance the aircraft was to be equipped with the GM-1 installation with a supply of 85 l of nitrous oxide, sufficient for about 17 minutes of continuous use.

The extended nose section of the fuselage housed a 64 liter oil tank installed to the right of the cannon. The front section of the steel tank featured additional 8 mm armor protection.

The Ta 152 A was to carry an engine-mounted MK 108 30 mm cannon with a supply of 75 to 80 rounds of ammunition. Additional armament was to include a pair of MG 151/20 20 mm cannons mounted on the top of the nose section (150 rounds per gun) and two wing-mounted MG 151/20 weapons with 175 rounds of ammunition per gun. The aircraft was also designed to accept two additional wing-mounted MK 108s (with 55 rounds per gun), or 2 MG 151/20 cannons, each with 140 rounds of ammunition. Alternatively, the fighter could carry external pods housing two MK 103 30 mm cannons with 40 rounds of ammunition per gun.

In the *Jabo* role the fighter could be armed with a single 500 kg general purpose bomb carried on a Schloß 503 bomb ejector attached to the centerline hardpoint. Similarly to the Fw 190 A, the aircraft had a capability to carry additional stores on wing stations, including various types of bomb ejectors or W.Gr. 21 tube launchers.

The assembly of the first three prototypes of the Ta 152 A began at Adelheide factory in 1943. All three machines were in fact modified Fw 190 A-0 airframes. The completed prototypes were then handed over to Focke-Wulf flight test facility (*Focke-Wulf Testzentrum*) at Hannover-Langenhagen. The first prototype to take to the skies was Fw 190 V 19, W.Nr. 0041, when it launched for its maiden flight on July 7, 1943. The aircraft was powered by the Jumo 213 A, Nr. 100 152 082, but it was soon discovered that the powerplant caused excessive airframe vibration operating at high rpm settings (around 3 250 rpm). The vibration continued even after the aircraft was re-engined with the Jumo 213 A, Nr. 100 152 160. It was not until the Jumo 213 CV, Nr. 100 1570 009 and the new VS 9 propeller were installed that the pesky vibration finally disappeared. On February 16, 1944 the aircraft was damaged in a landing accident caused by a failure of the landing gear locking mechanism. The damage was quickly repaired and the fighter soon rejoined the flight test program.

The Fw 190 V 19 originally featured the tail assembly from a standard Fw 190 D, which was later replaced with a unit designed for the Fw 190 C. The fuselage was extended by 0.5 m. The aircraft was unarmed, except for an engine-mounted MK 108 cannon which was added during the test program.

The second prototype of the Ta 152 A was Fw 190 V 20, W.Nr. 0042, TI+IG. The aircraft made its first flight on November 23, 1943 with Hans Sander at the controls. The fighter was powered by the Jumo 213 CV, Nr. 100 1570 010, driving the Schwartz VS 9 propeller. The prototype featured a 0.5 m fuselage extension and the C-type tail assembly. Similarly to its stable mate, the machine was unarmed. This particular aircraft was also used in the flame damper trials. The tests showed what Focke-Wulf engineers had already figured out: the aircraft equipped with flame dampers suffered a severe speed penalty. Without the flame dampers the fighter could achieve the top speed of 692 km/h at 7 000 m, which dropped to 657 km/h when the flame dampers were installed. On August 5, 1944 the prototype was severely damaged (over 70%) during an air raid on Langenhagen and was never repaired.

The "Einfach-Haube" did not perform well in trials and was soon replaced with an improved "Doppelhaube" cockpit design.

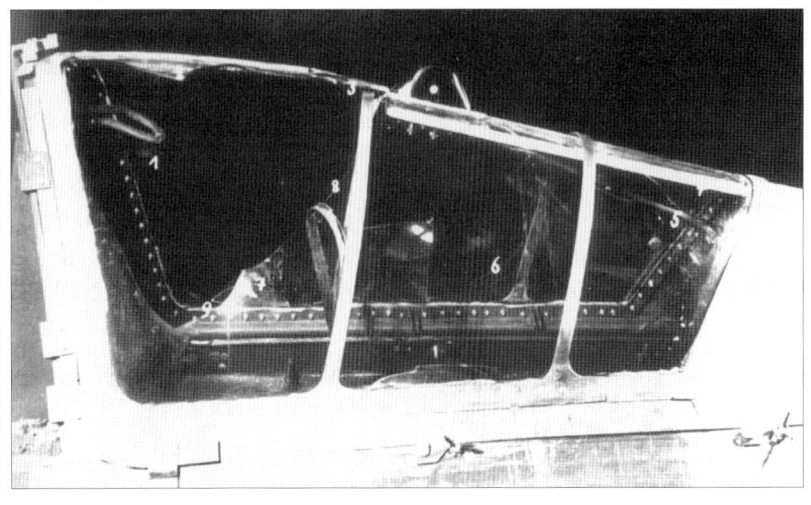

Another shot of the "Einfach-Haube" mock-up.

Development of the Ta 152 design

The "Doppelhaube" tested on the Fw 190 B-0 proved to be reliable. In this shot a Luftwaffe ace Hptm. Walter Nowotny is visiting Focke-Wulf plant on December 21, 1943 (Held).

Hptm. Walter Nowotny signing autographs during his visit to Focke-Wulf plant. The aircraft in the background is the Fw 190 B-0 (Held).

The last prototype of the Ta 152 A was Fw 190 V 21, W.Nr. 0043, TI+IH, first flown by Bernhard Märschel on March 13, 1944. The fighter was powered by the Jumo 213 CV, Nr. 100 1570 012, driving the Schwartz VS 9 propeller. Similarly to the other two prototypes, it was unarmed and featured a 0.5 m fuselage extension and the C-type tail assembly. The Fw 190 V 21 was initially used in trials of modified flame damper assemblies, but it soon became clear that the modifications did little to preserve the fighter's level flight speed performance. On May 5, 1944 the prototype was handed over to Erprobungsstelle Rechlin, where the test program continued.

Despite its excellent performance and glowing reports from the test pilots, the RLM did not authorized full scale production of the Ta 152 A and opted to continue the manufacturing of radial-powered Fw 190 As, whose performance above 5 000 m was greatly inferior to that promised by the Ta 152 A. What the RLM officials did authorize was a series production of the Fw 190 D models, which shared many design features with the Ta 152 A and used the Jumo 213 A inverted V engine.

In the fall of 1944 the RLM decided to discontinue the production of twin-engine Messerschmitt Me 410 destroyer aircraft in favor of single engine machines. To meet the RLM requirements, the Focke-Wulf engineers proposed the Ta 152 B-5 model powered by the Jumo 213 E engine and featuring additional MW 50 methanol-water injection system. The aircraft was to be armed with a single MK 103 cannon firing through the propeller hub and a pair of MK 103s mounted in the wing roots. The proposed design would feature heavy armor protection. The total weight of armor plating around the engine bay (10 and 6 mm plates) was 62 kg, while the cockpit armor (20, 15, 10, 8 and 5 mm plates) weighed in at 88 kg. The windshield design incorporated a 70 mm front plate, bringing the total weight of armor to 150 kg.

The fighter was to be equipped with FuG 16 ZY, FuG 25a and FuG 125 radios in addition to K 23 automatic pilot and Revi 16b reflector gun sight. Internal fuel would be carried in fuselage (594 l) and wing (470 l) fuel tanks. The fighter would also be able to carry an additional 300 l drop tank.

The Ta 152 B-5's top speed performance was calculated to be 529 km/h at sea level, 710 km/h at 9 500 m and 683 km/h at 10 700 m. Estimated range on internal fuel only was 1 165 km. The plans were in place to launch the full-scale production of the Ta 152 B-5 at Erla plant beginning in May 1945 and then, from July 1945, at Gotha factory.

The Fw 190 V 53, W.Nr. 170 003, DU+JC, originally used in trials of the Fw 190 D-9, was modified for tests of the wing-mounted MK 103 cannons. Under the designation of V 68 the prototype was sent to Erprobungsstelle Tarnewitz, where the weapons tests commenced on December 13, 1944.

The Ta 152 V 19, W.Nr. 110 019, Ta 152 V 20, W.Nr. 110 020 and Ta 152 V 21, W.Nr. 110 021 were to be used as prototypes of the Ta 152 B-5/R11 (an all-weather fighter equipped with the K 23 autopilot system). By the time the prototypes were assembled at Sorau factory Germany had practically lost the war and the test program never got off the ground.

In the final days of the war Focke-Wulf engineers prepared a preliminary project of a destroyer aircraft designated Ta 152 B-7. The fighter was to be powered by a Jumo 213 J featuring four valves per cylinder. The engine, equipped with a two-stage, three-speed supercharger was supposed to deliver 2 600 HP at take-off at 1 740 HP at 10 000 m.

Development of the Ta 152 design

Focke-Wulf Fw 190 B-0, W.Nr. 0046, TI+IK parked at Focke-Wulf factory airfield.

This Daimler-Benz DB 603 A-0 is ready for installation in the Focke-Wulf Fw 190 V 13.

The Ta 152 C was designed to operate at low and medium altitudes and was supposed to replace the Focke-Wulf Fw 190 A in that role. In early 1944 it became evident that the radial-powered Fw 190 A had reached the limits of its development potential. New generations of Allied fighters, including P-47 D Thunderbolt, P-51 D Mustang, Spitfire Mk. XIV or Tempest Mk. V could reach speeds approaching 700 km/h and quite easily outperformed the Focke-Wulf, which was some 40 to 50 km/h slower.

The Ta 152 C, with its inline Daimler-Benz DB 603L engine and the MW 50 water-methanol injection, was supposed to be the saving grace for struggling Luftwaffe aircrews. The aircraft was to be delivered in two versions: pure fighter (Ta 152 C-1) and fighter-bomber (Ta 152-C3).

The Ta 152 C was a single-engine, single-seat cantilever monoplane with retractable landing gear. The fuselage was largely a modified Ta 152 A structure. The front fuselage section was lengthened by 0.775 m to allow the installation of the MK 103 cannon and a pair of MG 152/20 weapons. Wing attachment points were moved forward by 0.420 m, which was necessary due to the altered CG. To properly balance the airframe the fuselage rear section was extended by the addition of a 0.5 m plug, which created additional space for oxygen bottles and compressed air tanks for operation of the engine-mounted cannon. The aircraft received a larger vertical stabilizer (1.77 sq m), but retained the original Fw 190 A-8 horizontal stabilizer assemblies.

Unlike production Fw 190 A featuring electrically operated landing gear retraction and extension system, the Ta 152 C had hydraulically actuated landing gear mechanism. The new fighter was heavier than the Fw 190 and it required larger main landing gear wheels (740 mm x 210 mm). The main landing gear

Focke-Wulf Fw 190 V 13, W.Nr. 0036, SK+JS photographed at Bremen airfield in March 1942.

Focke-Wulf Ta 152 — 11

Development of the Ta 152 design

Fw 190 V 13 was the first Fw 190 airframe to receive an inline engine – in this case the Daimler-Benz DB 603 A-0.

A right-side view of the Daimler-Benz DB 603 A-0.

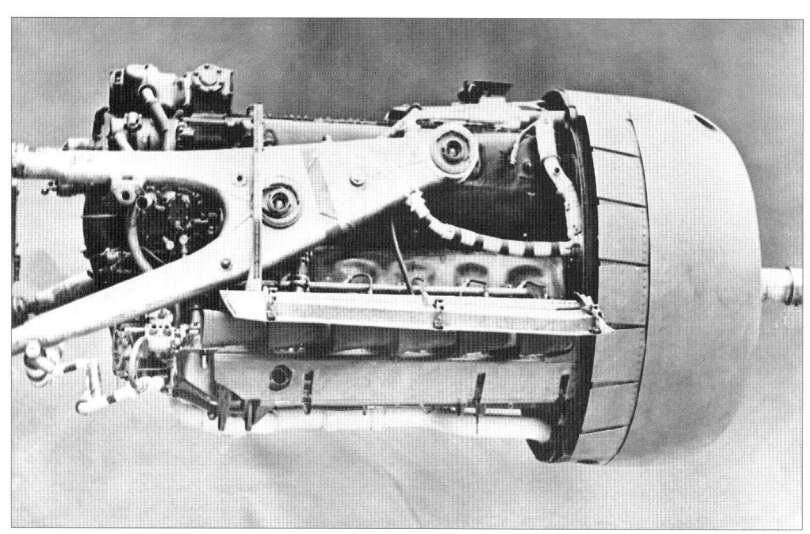

legs had to be moved outboard by 0.250 m, which meant the wingspan had to be increased from 10.5 m to 11.0 m. The aircraft featured completely redesigned wing to fuselage sections and strengthened wing skin panels.

Early production aircraft were to be powered by the Daimler-Benz DB 603 E rated at 1 750 HP, later to be replaced by the 1 870 HP DB 603 LA or DB 603 L.

The Ta 152 C's forward fuselage fuel tank holding 233 l of fuel was an unmodified Fw 190 A-8 unit, but it was installed slightly more forward due to changes introduced to the fuselage structure. The move allowed the installation of a larger aft fuel tank, which now had a capacity of 362 l. Both fuel tanks featured armor protection consisting of 16 mm plates covering bottom and side sections of the tanks and 12 mm plates on top of the tanks. The Ta 152 C-0, C-1 and C-3 models could also carry an additional 300 l drop tank on the centerline station. Additionally, the Ta 152 C-1 and C-3 were to feature bag tanks in the wings holding 470 l of fuel.

A 72 l oil tank was installed in the front section of the fuselage, just to the right of the cannon.

The Ta 152 C-1 was to be armed with a single MK 108 30 mm cannon firing through the propeller hub with a supply of 90 rounds of ammunition. In addition to the 30 mm weapon the aircraft would carry four 20 mm cannons: two MG 151/20s mounted on top of the nose (150 rounds per gun) and a pair of MG 151/20 cannons installed in the wing roots (175 rounds of ammunition per gun). The offensive armament of the C-3 version was supposed to include an MK 108 30 mm cannon mounted between the cylinder blocks (with 80 rounds of ammunition) and four MG 151/15 weapons installed on top the nose (150 rounds per gun) and in the wing roots (175 rounds per gun). The *Jabo* variant (Ta 152 C-3) would have the capability to carry a single bomb (up to 500 kg) on the Schloß 503 bomb ejector.

The Ta 152 C's radio suite consisted of the FuG 16 ZY radio, FuG 25a IFF set, FuG 125 navigational radio and K 23 autopilot.

Initial plans called for the construction of 17 prototypes, 16 of which were to be assembled from scratch. The seventeenth prototype was to be a redesigned Fw 190 V 21 with a new

Development of the Ta 152 design

designation of Fw 190 V21/U 1. However, by the time those plans were made Germany was already losing the war and the proposed new prototypes were never built.

The first prototype in the Ta 152 C-1 program was the Fw 190 V 21/ U 1, W.Nr. 0043, TI+IH powered by the Daimler-Benz DB 603 E, W.Nr.525. The aircraft first flew on November 3, 1944 with Bernhard Märschel at the controls. Later on the same day Märschel flew the prototype from Adelheide to Langenhagen, where it was handed over to Deimler-Benz engineers. On November 19, 1944 Fw. Albrecht ferried the aircraft to Deimler-Benz factory airfield at Echterdingen for installation of the new DB 603 LA V 16 powerplant. Flight test program of the new engine began on December 10, 1944 and continued through March, 1945.

The next Ta 152 C prototypes were assembled at Sorau (today's Żary). The first aircraft to make its maiden flight was the Ta 152 V 6, W.Nr. 110 006, VH+EY. The fighter, powered by the Daimler-Benz DB 603 EC, W.Nr. 0130 0145 and equipped with a V 19 propeller and MW 50 boost, was first flown by Bernhard Märschel on December 12, 1944. Some of the prototype's features included larger wing (19.5 sq m) spanning 11.0 m, heated canopy side panels, wooden trailing edge flaps and ETC 503 ejector on the centerline station. The aircraft was armed with a pair of MG 151 cannons on top of the nose and two MG 151s installed in the wing roots. The fighter, weighing in at 4 370 kg, was to be the prototype of the Ta 152 C-0.

During the flight test program the prototype reached the top speed of 547 km/h at sea level (2500 rpm and 1.45 atm. boost pressure) at 647 km/h at 6 850 m. At war emergency power settings (*Sondernotleistung* – 2 700 rpm and 1.95 atm. boost pressure) the top sea level speed increased to 617 km/h, while at 5 250 m the aircraft could reach 687 km/h.

The next prototype was first flown by Bernhard Märschel on January 8, 1945. The Ta 152 V 7, W.Nr. 110 007, CI+XM was powered by the Daimler-Benz DB 603 EC, Nr. 0130 0147 and equipped with the MW 50 boost. On January 16, 1945 Märschel flew the aircraft from Adelheide to Langenhagen, where the aircraft was flight tested on three occasions (January 27, February 3 and February 6, 1945) by Hans Sander. In March 1945 the aircraft received the Daimler-Benz DB 603 LA powerplant.

The armament consisted of two fuselage-mounted MG 151 cannons and a pair of MG 151s installed in the wing roots. The machine was also equipped with the K 23 autopilot, since it was supposed to be the prototype of an all-weather fighter version – the Ta 152 C-1/R 11. There were plans to transfer the aircraft to Erprobungsstelle Gotenhafen-Hexengrund

A top view of the DB 603 A-0.

(today's Gdynia), where it was supposed to be modified to carry airborne torpedoes. However, by the time the flight test program at Langenhagen was completed, the Goteshafen facility had been captured by Soviet troops.

The Ta 152 V 8, W.Nr. 110 008, GW+QA powered by the Daimler-Benz DB 603 EC, W.Nr. 0130 0150 and featuring the MW 50 boost was first flown by Bernhard Märschel on January 15, 1945. On January 20, 1945 Märschel ferried the fighter from Adelheide to Langenhagen. The prototype was fitted identically to the previous examples and carried the same armament suite. The only difference was the installation of the Askania Adler Revi EZ 42 reflector gun sight. In February 1945 the aircraft underwent trials at Erprobungsstelle Rechlin.

The next series of prototype machines never proceeded beyond the drawing board. The aircraft were supposed to be the definite prototypes of the production Ta 152 C-1 versions equipped with integral fuel tanks (470 l capacity) and a full armament fit consisting of a sin-

The DB 603 A-0 installed in the Focke-Wulf Fw 190 V 13 (view from the right side).

Development of the Ta 152 design

The DB 603 A-0 installed in the Fw 190 V 13 (view from the left side).

Fw 190 V 13 equipped with a mock-up of the ETC ejector.

gle MK 108 30 mm cannon firing through the propeller hub and four MG 151/20 20 mm weapons. The production of the first three machines (Ta 152 V 10, V 11 and V 12, W.Nr. 110 010 to 110 012) was cancelled as early as October 18, 1944. The Ta 152 V 13, W.Nr. 110 013 and Ta 152 V 15, W.Nr. 110 015 were supposed to be powered by the DB 603 L. The same power plant was to be used in the V 16, W.Nr. 110 016, V 17, W.Nr. 110 017 and V 18, W.Nr. 110 018. Additionally, those three aircraft were to be equipped with the FuG 15 radio in place of the FuG 16 ZY set as prototypes of the Ta 152 C-3 version. Various sources place the cancellation date of those aircraft either on December 28, 1944, or as late as April or May, 1945.

Most likely none of the three Ta 152 C-4 prototypes were ever built. The aircraft, powered by the DB 603 L, was supposed to be equipped with the FuG 15 radio and fuselage mounted MG 151/20 20 mm cannon in place of the MK 108. The never completed machines included the Ta 152 V 22, W.Nr. 110 022, Ta 152 V 23, W.Nr. 110 023 and Ta 152 V 24, W.Nr. 110 024.

Two other aircraft that were used in the Ta 152 C-3 program were the Ta 152 H-0 prototypes – the Ta 152 V 27, W.Nr. 150 027 and Ta 152 V 28, W.Nr. 150 030. Both machines were supposed to receive the DB 603 E powerplants and MW 50 boost. However, due to time constraints the aircraft remained in their original

Development of the Ta 152 design

Focke-Wulf Fw 190 V 15, W.Nr. 0037, CF+OV made its first flight on May 9, 1942 with Hans Sander at the controls. Initially the aircraft was powered by the DB 603 A-0, which was later replaced with the DB 603 A-1.

configuration. The Ta 152 V 27 received a new serial, W.Nr. 150 030, before it was first flown by Hans Sander on February 2, 1945. Later on the same day the aircraft was destroyed in a crash at Langenhagen. The Ta 152 V 28 was probably ready to begin flight test program in mid February 1945. Similarly to its sister ship, the fighter received a new serial – W.Nr. 150 031.

Production Ta 152 C-1/R11 aircraft were supposed to be initially powered by the DB 603 E powerplant, which was to be replaced later by the DB 603 L featuring a two stage supercharger

This photograph of the Fw 190 V 15 clearly shows an air duct directing exhaust gasses into the compressor (not yet installed).

Development of the Ta 152 design

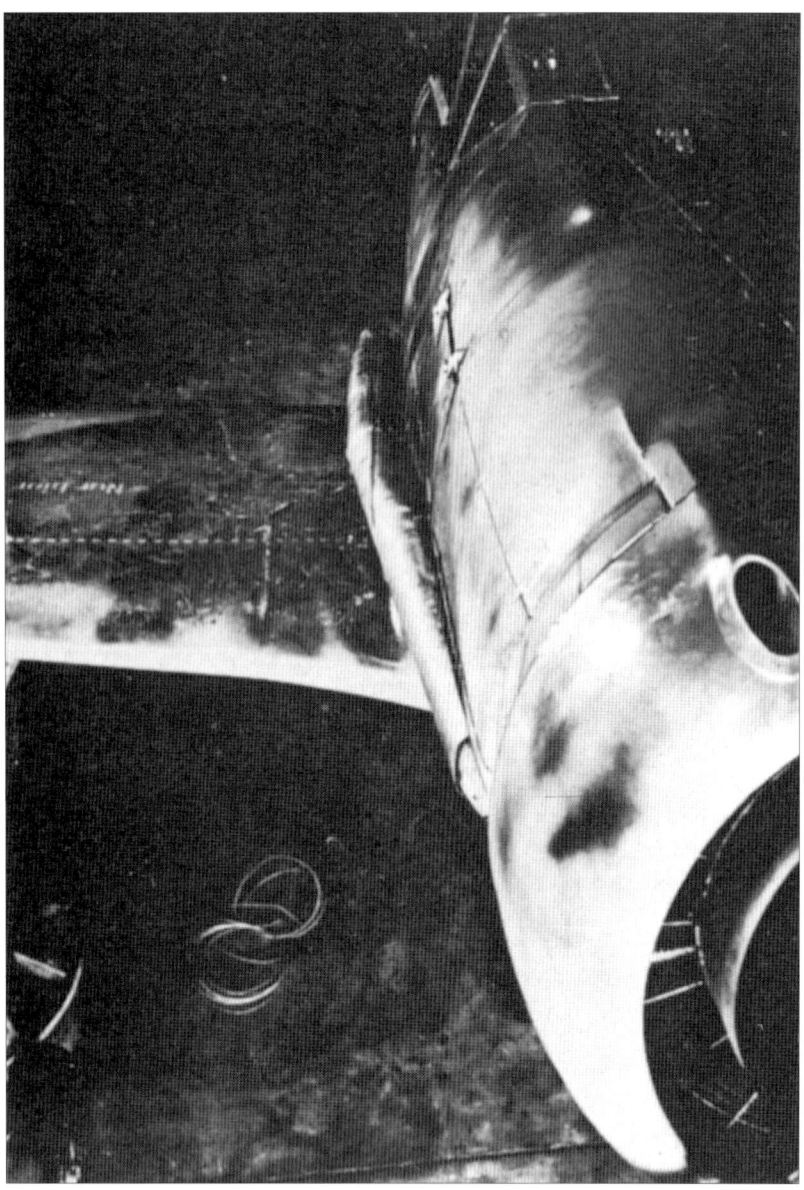

Air duct and associated fairing feeding exhaust gasses into the compressor installed on the Fw 190 V 15.

with an intercooler system. There were plans to launch the full-scale production of the Ta 152 C-1/R11 in March 1945. The aircraft were to be assembled at ATG plant in Leipzig (serials beginning with W.Nr. 920 001) and at Siebel in Halle (serials beginning with 360 001 and, most probably with W.Nr. 440 001). Additionally, one of the Ta 152 C-1/R11 was to be manufactured at MMW-Mimetallwerke in Erfurt (serials from W.Nr. 870 001 or 950 001 as the C-11/R11 version).

There were further plans to launch the production of the Ta 152 C-1 at Arbeits-Gemeinschaft Roland Leipzig (serials from W.Nr. 790 001) and at Gotha plant (serials from W.Nr. 720 001). However, by the time the manufacturing was supposed to begin (May 1945) the war was already over.

Both the C-0 and the C-1 versions of the Ta 152 could be delivered in the R11 configuration, i.e. all-weather fighter. The R11 modifications included the installation of FuG 123 radios and LGW K autopilot, as well as the addition of heated canopy side panels. The C-1 variant featured fuselage mounted MK 108 30 mm cannon and four 151/20 20 mm weapons. The C-3 carried the MK 103 cannon firing through the propeller hub in addition to four MG 151/15 15 mm cannons. The C-2 and C-4 variants were to be equipped with FuG 15 radios in place of the FuG 16 ZY sets. The C-5 variant was to be armed with five MG 151/20 20 mm cannons, but the planned armament fit was later changed to include a single fuselage mounted MK 103 with a pair of identical weapons installed in the wing roots. The C-11/R11 was a variant of the C-1/R11 which was based on the reconnaissance Ta 152 E-1 airframe.

One of the more interesting Ta 152 C-1 versions was a torpedo aircraft designated Ta 152 C-1/R14. The initial plans were drafted following a requirement for a torpedo-carrying version of the Ta 152 C, which was issued by the RLM on December 12, 1944.

On January 24, 1945 the Luftwaffe High Command (*Oberkommando der Luftwaffe* – OKL) placed an order for standard and high-altitude reconnaissance versions of the Ta 152 C. The standard reconnaissance aircraft, designated Ta 152 E-1, was to be a successor of the Bf 109 G models used in the reconnaissance role by frontline Luftwaffe units. The aircraft was to be powered by the Jumo 213 E engine and fitted with FuG 15 and FuG 25a radios. The armament was to be limited to a single fuselage mounted MK 108 cannon and two MG 151/20 20 mm cannons in the wing roots. The fighter would also feature bag tanks in the wings and a capability to carry a 300 l drop tank attached to a Schloß 503 ejector. Installed inside the fuselage would be a tank holding methanol-water mixture used in the MW 50 boost installation, or, alternatively, an additional 115 l fuel tank. The aircraft could carry a variety of photographic cameras, including Rb 75/30, Rb 50/30, Rb 30/18 or Rb 50/18. It could also used mixed camera sets, such as 2xRb 20/12x12, 2xRb 40/12x12, 2xRb 12,5/7x9 or 2xRb 32/7x9. A Robot II camera was to be installed in the leading edge of the port wing. A Voigtländer Durchblickfernrohr 67 G unit was to be used to cover the area directly below the aircraft. Of the more interesting variants was the Ta 152 E-1/R1, which featured an oblique installation of an Rb 50/18 tilted at a 10° angle.

If the aircraft's fuselage was to hold different types of photographic sensors in addition to the MW 50 mixture and/or additional fuel, changes to the basic structure were necessary. Frames 9 and 10 were moved forward and modified to accept photographic equipment. The camera bay access panel located on the left side of the fuselage was enlarged and moved to a slightly different location. The FuG 25a set was also moved to the back to make room for

Development of the Ta 152 design

the cameras. The ADF antenna was installed between frames 8 and 9. Heavy camera equipment installed in the aft section of the fuselage made the aircraft tail heavy, so the compressed air bottles were moved forward in order to restore proper balance. Additional two-liter compressed air tank was installed in the left wing root for emergency flaps and landing gear operation. Another, five-liter tank provided compressed air for operation of the MK 108 cannon. A single two-liter compressed air gas was also installed in the right wing root and was used for emergency services operation (flaps/landing gear). In the same place three oxygen bottles were also installed.

The aircraft's range could be increased if an additional 115 l fuel tank was carried in place of the GM-1 or MW 50 boost systems. Additional 300 liters of fuel could be carried in an external drop tank.

The 152 V 9, W.Nr. 110 009 and Ta 152 V 14, W.Nr. 110 014 were planned to be used as prototypes of the reconnaissance version. Both aircraft were to be powered by the Jumo 213 E with MW 50 boost. The machines were planned to be completed by 18 and 25 January, 1945, but on January 5 the RLM instructed Focke-Wulf to abandon the project. Instead a decision was made to use the first production example of the Ta 152 E in tests of the new equipment. The reconnaissance version was scheduled to go into full-scale production at MMW-Mimetallwerke beginning in February 1945. The first production batch of thirty aircraft would not be equipped with the Durchblickfernrohr installation. Due to some production delays the first production example of the Ta 152 E-1 was not ready until March 1, 1945. It was generally feared that the increased weight of the aircraft carrying up to 70 kg of photographic equipment would have a significant impact on the fighter's stability. There are no archival sources available to confirm if and when the machine was actually flight tested. In the meantime, due to deterio-

Another shot of the air duct directing exhaust gasses into the compressor installed on the Fw 190 V 15.

Cockpit of the Fw 190 V 15. On the central console, just below the main instrument panels, are coolant temperature and oil temperature indicators.

Development of the Ta 152 design

A close-up shot of the left side of the engine cowl installed on the Fw 190 V 16, W.Nr. 0038, CF+OW.

Another shot of the same aircraft, this time taken from the right.

rating situation on the frontlines, the unfinished airframes were used in the assembly of additional Ta 152 C models, which were completed as the C-11 variants.

The proposed high-altitude version of the reconnaissance platform was originally designated Ta 152 E-2, which was later changed to Ta 152 H-10. The aircraft, based on the Ta 152 H-1 airframe, was supposed to have a high aspect ratio wing (23.5 m wing span), pressurized cockpit and GM-1 installation providing extra boost for about 17 minutes. The prototype of the high-altitude reconnaissance version was to be the Ta 152 V26, W.Nr. 110 021, CW+CU, a standard Ta 152 H-0 or H-1 airframe converted for the new role at the MMW plant in Erfurt. The aircraft W.Nr. 150 167, which was later captured by the U.S. forces in Erfurt, was to be used in the same role.

The armament of the proposed reconnaissance version was to be identical as the Ta 152 H-1 model: one MK 108 30 mm cannon firing through the propeller hub with a supply of 85 rounds of ammunition and a pair of MG 151/20s with 220 rounds of ammunition per gun. The avionics would include FuG 15 and FuG 25a radio sets. The aircraft was to be equipped with internally mounted oblique Robot Rb 75/30 camera coupled with a 67 G (Durchblickfernrohr 67 G) telescopic viewfinder.

It is perhaps worthwhile at this point to mention some of the specialized armament configurations planned for the Ta 152. One of them included underwing installation of wooden launchers (12 per wing) for R4M unguided rockets. The R4Ms were used by Messerschmitt Me 262 A jets and Focke-Wulf Fw 190 D-9 fighters from Jagdgruppe 10 based at Parchim. The Ta 152 variants with the R4M capability were to be designated Ta 152 C-1/R31 and Ta 152 H-1/R31.

Another weapon planned for installation on the Ta 152 was the *Sondergerät 500* – "special device 500", or, as it was often called, the *Jägerfaust* – "fighter's fist". It was a recoilless weapon firing SG 500 heavy 50 mm projectiles. There were plans to install five upward-pointing SG 500 tubes in each wing of the Ta 152 in place of one of the wing tanks. Operation of the weapon was fully automatic. To attack an enemy bomber the pilot had to approach the target from below and position his aircraft within the shadow cast by the bomber. The shadow was detected by a photube, which activated the SG 500 trigger mechanism. At some point the weapon was tested on an Fw 190 at Waffenerprobungsstelle Tarnewitz.

There were also plans to develop a two-seat trainer designated Ta 152 S-1, which was to be based on the Ta 152 C-1 airframe powered by the DB 603. The redesigned fuselage assemblies, housing an additional cockpit and associated equipment, were to be manufactured by Blohm & Voss from April 1945. Later on, in August 1945, the production of the two-seat version was also to be launched at DHL (Deutsche Lufthansa) plant in Prague. The trainers would not carry any armament. The first Ta 152 S prototype was supposed to be ready by November 1944, but it never saw the light of day due to significant delays marring the entire Ta 152 program. Erprobungsstelle Rechlin recommended that at least 3 percent of production Ta 152 C aircraft should be delivered in the two-seat version. There were plans to manufacture as many as 565 Ta 152 S-1s by March 1946.

Beginning in late 1944 the Focke-Wulf design team concentrated on further development of the Ta 152 H. It was proposed that the aircraft's successor should feature a new engine (Junkers Jumo 222 E) and a re-designed, laminar-flow wing. The airframe design should allow the use of either Jumo 222 E or Jumo 222 A powerplants.

The Jumo 222 was initially designed to power a new generation of Luftwaffe bombers, including the Ju 288 – a future replacement of the Ju 88. Jumo 222 E was a 24-cylinder engine displacing 4 985 ccm rated at 2 900 HP with MW 50 boost. The engine drove a three-bladed wooden Junkers VS 19 propeller. Equipped with this engine-propeller combination the Ta 152 H could carry up to 1 072 l of B4 avgas (232 l in forward fuselage tank, 360 l in the aft tank and 240 l in each integral wing tank).

The aircraft was to receive a new laminar-flow wing featuring two main spars. The wing, spanning 13.68 m, would have the area of 23.80 sq m. The aircraft's take-off weight was calculated at 5 815 kg.

The proposed fighter was to be armed with two fuselage mounted MG 151/20 cannons (150 rounds of ammunition per gun) and a pair of identical weapons installed in the wing roots with a supply of 175 rounds of ammunition per gun. Alternatively, the fighter would be able to carry two fuselage mounted MG 151/20s supplemented by two MK 103 30 mm cannons in the wing roots with 55 rounds per gun. The fighter would feature armor protection around the engine bay and in various parts of the fuselage weighing in at 157 kg. The avionics suite was to include FuG 16 ZY radio, FuG 25a set, FuG 125 receiver, K 23 autopilot and Revi 16b reflector gun sight.

The fighter's top speed at 9 500 m was calculated at 710 km/h with the use of MW 50 boost. At sea level the aircraft was supposed to climb at 22 m/s. The operating ceiling was estimated at 15 000 m, while the range at a cruising altitude of 10 500 was calculated at 1 290 km (without the 300 l drop tank).

To facilitate the design process and flight testing of a wide range of planned Ta 152 versions, a decision was made in the summer of 1944 to build no fewer than 26 prototype aircraft to be used in the Ta 152 program. All airframes were to be assembled by the Sorau plant. The construction of the Ta 152 A-1 prototypes (Ta 152 V1 and V2) was very quickly abandoned, similarly to the V3, V4 and V5 aircraft to be used as the Ta 152 H-1 prototypes. See Appendices for a list of all experimental Ta 152 aircraft built at Sorau.

The Fw 190 V 16, W.Nr. 0038, CF+OW was first flown in the summer of 1942.

Focke-Wulf Ta 152 H high-altitude fighter

When the Höhenjäger 2 program was launched at Focke-Wulf the company intended to build six prototypes of the new fighter. The first to be completed was the modified Fw 190 V 18, which first flew on December 20, 1942 as Fw 190 V 18/U1, W.Nr. 0040, CF+OY. The maiden flight took place at company airfield in Bremen with Hans Sander at the controls. The prototype had neither the pressurized cockpit,

The Fw 190 V 16 undergoing trials at Echterdingen airfield.

During the tests at Echterdingen the Fw 190 V 16 reached a top speed of 722 km/h at 9 000 m.

nor the new, longer wing spanning 12.30 m. It was equipped with FuG VIIa and FuG 25 radios and was powered by the DB 603 A-1 engine driving a four bladed, metal propeller (the engine originally planned for the prototype, the DB 603 G, had not been available yet). The metal propeller was later replaced with a wooden unit. The aircraft was equipped with the TK 9 AC turbocharger developed by the *Deutsche Versuchsanstalt für Luftfahrt* – DVL and by Hirth aero engine company. Mounted under the fuselage, the 240 kg unit worked at 2 200 rpm with the inlet gas temperature of 950°C. Exhaust gasses were directed into the turbocharger via two ducts running along each side of the fuselage. The gas turbine was located under the

Characteristic air scoops feeding coolant and oil radiators installed on the Fw 190 V 16.

rear section of the fuselage. Compressed air was directed into a radiator unit with a frontal area of 0.81 sq m.

During initial speed trials Hans Sander accelerated the aircraft to 494 km/h at sea level and 680 km/h at 11 000 m. Despite those rather impressive results, Sander did not like the new design. The aircraft was very unstable in all three axes and was a handful to fly. The CG was located so far back that it was impossible to properly trim the machine below 7 700 m. During landing, the tail-heavy aircraft displayed a tendency to touch down tail wheel first, which caused all kinds of ground handling issues. The Fw 190 V18/U1 flight test program was completed on November 26, 1943 after the aircraft had flown 66 sorties.

The next batch of prototypes (Fw 190 V 29, V 30, V 31, V 32 and V 33) received larger wings (20.3 sq m) – the so called *Parise Fläche*, or "Parisian wings" (a suitable nickname given the fact that they were manufactured by a factory in occupied France). All aircraft were powered by the DB 603 S-1 engine (a modified version of the DB 603 A-1) and featured the TK 11 turbocharger. They also had pressurized cockpits and FuG 16 and FuG 25a radios.

Fw 190 V 29, W.Nr. 0054, GH+KS, W.Nr. 1717801 was first flown on February 27, 1943. On June 27, 1943 the aircraft was delivered to

The Focke-Wulf Fw 190 V 18/U1, W.Nr. 0040, CF+OY was the first prototype of the Höhenjäger 2.

The Fw 190 V 18/U1 featured pressurized cockpit, a turbocharger and a four-bladed propeller.

Focke-Wulf Ta 152 H high-altitude fighter

A close-up shot of the pressurized cockpit and the air duct directing exhaust gasses into the turbocharger installed on the Fw 190 V18/U1.

Fw 190 V 18/U1 parked in front of Focke-Wulf's assembly building at Bremen.

Hirth for engine and turbocharger trials. The Fw 190 V 30, W.Nr. 0055, GH+KT made its maiden flight on March 7, 1943. It later underwent engine trials at Hirth using two different powerplants: DB 603 S-1, W.Nr. 1717803 and 1717815. In each case the engines drove a four-bladed wooden propeller. Before delivery to Erprobungsstelle Rechlin for further trials, the aircraft had received a new high-altitude magneto system and re-designed oil cooler. The Fw 190 V 31, W.Nr. 0056, GH+KU first flew on April 5, 1943. On May 28, 1943, during one of the test sorties, the aircraft flown by Werner Bartsch developed engine problems. The pilot attempted a forced landing near Kaltenweide, but on roll-out the fighter nosed over and was completely destroyed. The Fw 190 V 32, W.Nr. 0057, GH+KV carried offensive armament consisting of a pair of wing-mounted MG 151/20s. After its maiden flight the aircraft was re-engined with the DB 603 G powerplant and handed over to Daimler-Benz for further trials.

Focke-Wulf Ta 152 H high-altitude fighter

The Fw 190 V 18/U1 equipped with the TK 11 turbocharger under the fuselage.

The Fw 190 V 18/U1 was powered by the Daimler-Benz DB 603 S-1.

The last prototype to be built was the Fw 190 V 33, W.Nr. 0058, GH+KW, which made its first flight on May 7, 1943. Similarly to the V 32 the aircraft featured two wing-mounted MG 151/20 cannons. After its first flight the prototype was handed over to Erprobungsstelle Rechlin, where the test program continued.

One of the Rechlin test pilots, Heinrich Beauvais, had an opportunity to fly one of the prototypes: "On March 27, 1943 Hans Sander arrived at Rechlin in an Fw 190 prototype powered by the DB 603 and equipped with the TK 11 turbocharger. He didn't have much time, as he wanted to go back to Bremen as soon as possible. I was therefore in a bit of a rush and, during the take-off roll, attempted to get the aircraft flying from a three-point attitude. We adopted that take-off technique from frontline units, but used it only occasionally and always with a lot of caution. Well, in that particular instant it almost ended in a disaster: right after becoming airborne, the aircraft suddenly dropped the starboard wing, despite my immediate response with full rudder deflection. For a split second I was completely at the plane's mercy. I remember thinking: 'It's just stalled'. I instinctively kicked the left rudder, while at the same time giving the stick a short, but energetic shove forward. I managed to plant the main landing gear back on the ground in what was a rather soft and gentle touchdown. I then waited for the airspeed to build up and took-off without further incidents. Nobody on the ground seemed to have noticed anything unusual."[1]

The Hirth TK 11 turbine did not deliver the expected results. The Höhenjäger 2 prototypes equipped with the device had greatly degraded handling characteristics and the additional drag created by the radiator exacted a 40 to 50 km/h speed penalty.

Focke-Wulf Ta 152 H high-altitude fighter

The Fw 190 V 18/U1 seen from behind.

In the summer of 1943 Focke-Wulf engineers began work on another high-altitude Fw 190 variant, referred to in the company documents as Fw 190 Ra-6. Under its official designation of Fw 190 H the new fighter was to feature a larger and longer wing. Standard Fw 190 wings spanned 10.5 m and had a wing area of 18.3 sq m. The wing designed for the Fw 190 H was longer (14.8 m) and had a wing area of 22.5 sq m). The new wing's internal structure remained unchanged. The aircraft's fuselage was a standard Wf 190 B assembly modified with an extension plug. The airframe was designed to accept a variety of powerplants, including the Daimler-Benz DB 603 G, DB 627 and DB 632 or Junkers Jumo 213 E. While the DB 603 G and Jumo 213 E were at that time mass-produced and readily available, the DB 627 was much harder to come by with only a few test examples of the engine having been manufactured. The DB 632 project never proceeded beyond the drawing board.

The optimistic design team at Focke-Wulf calculated the Ta 152 H top speed to be somewhere from 695 to 740 km/h, depending on the installed powerplant model. The calculations assumed the use of GM-1 system at cruising altitudes of 11 000 to 13 000 m. The aircraft was to be armed with an engine-mounted MK 108 cannon and two MG151/20s in the wing roots.

Three prototypes of the new fighter were to be built. In order to save time, the company decided to use the existing airframes originally built for the Höhenjäger 2 program. The first machine to be modified as a Fw 190 H prototype was the Fw 190 V 32, W.Nr. 0057, GH+KV. The turbocharger and associated exhaust gas ducts were removed. The machine was powered by a DB 603 S-1 engine driving a wooden, four bladed Schwarz 9-41247.10 propeller. Unarmed aircraft weighed in at 3 940 kg.

The Fw 190 V 32 made its first flight in a new configuration on November 11, 1943 with Focke-Wulf company test pilot, Werner Kampmeier at the controls. A month later the airframe received a 0.5 m fuselage extension plug. During one of the test sorties the aircraft reach the top speed of 686 km/h at 6 750 m using the engine's full military power (2 500 rpm). In March 1944 prof. Kurt Tank personally flew two sorties in the Fw 190 V 32 launching from Langenhagen airfield. Between May 9 and May 12, 1944 the prototype underwent high-altitude tests at Erprobungsstelle Rechlin. After the trials the aircraft was delivered to Echterdingen for tests of new Deimler-Benz powerplants, the DB 603 E and DB 603 G.

The flight test program demonstrated that the aircraft still had rather poor handling characteristics and some serious longitudinal stability issues, despite the use of a larger, C-type stabilizer and the 0.5 m fuselage plug. There were also some stability problems in the pitch axis.

The Fw 190 V 32 was very difficult to fly in variable wind conditions. The large, four-bladed propeller pulled the aircraft's nose down making ground handling rather tricky. On the upside, cockpit pressurization system worked as advertised and maintained cabin pressure equivalent to 5 900 m while cruising at 10 000 m. The flight test program was very intense, which meant some systems (e.g. windshield defog and sprinkler systems) were not tested until April 6, 1944, after 41 flight test sorties had been flown.

The next two prototypes (Fw 190 V 30 and V 33) were to be powered by the new Junkers Jumo 213 E engine in place of the Daimler-Benz powerplant. Another aircraft to join the Ta 152

Focke-Wulf Ta 152 H high-altitude fighter

This photograph of the Fw 190 V 18/U1 shows the large vertical fin to good advantage.

H program was the Fw 190 V 32, which was delivered to Adelheide by Hans Sander on August 15, 1944. There the aircraft was to be converted to the Ta 152 H standard.

In December 1943 Focke-Wulf began work on a new high-altitude fighter design designated Ta 152 H. Focke-Wulf designers hoped that the new machine would beat the Bf 109 H as the preferred high-altitude asset in service with the Luftwaffe units. The Messerschmitt's bid, based on the Bf 109 G airframe, proved to be an unsuccessful design. It was originally designed as an interceptor of high-flying Allied reconnaissance aircraft. The first trials of the prototype, Bf 109 V 54, PV+JB, began on November 5, 1943. The aircraft received wing root extensions, which increased the wing span to 13.26 m and the wing area to 21.9 sq m (a standard Bf 109 G had a wing span of 9.924 m and the wing area of 16.2 sq m). The aircraft featured a larger fin and wider track landing gear. Soon a second prototype joined the test program (the Bf 109 V 55 PV+JC). The Messerschmitt's new fighter could reach the speed of 580 km/h with GM-1 boost at 12 600 m. During test sorties it became clear that the aircraft was very unstable around all three axes. Additionally, the long wing showed a tendency to buffet and vibrate in the least predictable moments. It was therefore not long before the RLM cancelled the plans for full-scale production of the aircraft. The role of the ill-fated design was partially fulfilled by another Messerschmitt design – the Bf 109 K-2/R2, which had a quite satisfactory high-altitude performance.

On December 7, 1943 the RLM place an order for six prototypes of the Ta 152 H fighter. In order for the new machine to enter full-

The Fw 190 V 18/U1 parked at Focke-Wulf's factory airfield at Bremen.

Focke-Wulf Ta 152 H high-altitude fighter

The Fw 190 V 18/U1 undergoing conversion at Adelheide.

scale production in the shortest possible time, the design was to be based on the Focke-Wulf Fw 190 A-8 used by the Luftwaffe. In fact, the RLM officials were particularly interested in the Ta 152 C version featuring high aspect ratio wing, pressurized cockpit plus GM-1 and MW 50 boost systems. The armament was to be reduced to a single fuselage mounted MK 108 cannon and two MG 151/20s installed in the wing roots. The powerplant chosen for the new design was Junkers Jumo 213 E. The aircraft was to be equipped with FuG 16 ZY and FuG 25a radios.

The first Ta 152 H prototype was a modified Fw 190 V33/U1 airframe, W.Nr. 0058, GH+KW, which first flew on July 12, 1944. The aircraft was powered by Junkers Jumo 213 E driving a three-bladed VS 9 propeller. The round-tipped wing had a span of 14.82 m and the wing area of 23.5 sq m. The main landing gear featured large wheels (740 x 240 mm), while the fuselage nose section was extended by 0.775 m. Also the aft section of the fuselage was lengthened by the addition of a 0.5 m fuselage plug. The bulged engine cover in front of the windshield was there to allow installation of a pair of MG 151/20 cannons. The V33 however, was not armed. Neither did it carry engine boost installations. On July 13, 1944 the aircraft was completely destroyed in a forced landing incident during a repositioning sortie from Adelheide to Langenhagen. Following the crash, the CO of Erprobungsstelle Rechlin, Obstlt. Edgar Petersen, sent a letter to the RLM's Technical Department requesting the construction of as many as twelve prototype machines, the number which Petersen considered a minimum for proper testing of the new design.

The second prototype, the Fw 190 V 30/U1, W.Nr. 0055, GH+KT, made its maiden flight on August 6, 1944. During the test program the machine spent a total of 10 hours and 3 minutes in the air. During high-altitude sorties It was discovered that the supercharger's third stage failed to engage and that there was a drop in fuel pressure above 9 000 m. The reason for the latter soon proved to be the fuel pumps that were not designed for operation at high altitudes. On August 19, 1944 the aircraft was taken through its paces by test pilots at Erprobungsstelle Rechlin. During one of high-altitude sorties, on August 23, 1944, the Jumo 213 E engine caught fire. Since the fire did not spread beyond the engine bay area, Flugkapitän Alfred Thomas opted to stay with the machine and bring it back for an emergency landing at Adelheide. The aircraft entered Adelheide's pattern and then suddenly dropped a wing and impacted the ground killing the pilot. Hans Sander witnessed the crash from the ground: "Having suffered the engine fire during a high-altitude sortie, the V 30/U1 crashed on its approach to land. We had no radio contact with the pilot, so that's about all we managed to find out."[2]

By September 20, 1944 the third prototype was ready. The Fw 190 V 29/U1, W.Nr.

Having completed the turbocharger test program the Fw 190 V 29, W.Nr. 0054, GH+KS was used as one of the Ta 152 prototypes.

26

The Focke-Wulf Fw 190 V 30, W.Nr. 005, GH+KT was later converted into one of the Ta 152 prototypes.

0054, GH+KS first flew three days later, on September 23, 1944 piloted by the Focke-Wulf chief test pilot Hans Sander. The aircraft had the fuselage mounted MG 151/20 cannons removed and featured a wing with square wingtips, which spanned 14.44 m. The prototype's flight test program began in earnest on November 3, 1944. During one of the sorties the fighter flown by Ofw. Friedrich Schnier reached a record-breaking altitude of 13 654 m. "Before I made that record flight", remembers Schnier, "I had never flown above 11 000 m. That particular sortie was supposed to demonstrated the highest altitude that the Ta 152 H was capable of reaching. The standard altimeters that we were using at that time were calibrated up to 12 000 m, so the aircraft was fitted with an additional Italian-made instrument that could read up to 14 000 m. The altimeter was carefully checked and calibrated both before and after the flight. The initial climb was fairly standard and I made standard calls every 1 000 m of altitude (reporting airspeed, altitude, cabin pressure and temperature). At 10 000 m I tried to pressurize the cockpit by inflating the rubber seal, but the result was less than satisfactory. The cabin pressure remained only slightly higher than the pressure outside. Above 10 000 m I felt itching and then pain in my knees and elbows. At the same time I had a feeling that my limbs were becoming stiff. Once I passed 12 000 m I made a call to let folks on the ground know that my standard altimeter had just run out of scale. I continued the slow ascent all the while being very aware of the fact that I had never flown that high before. The visibility was getting worse and worse, almost like watching a movie in a cinema. The sky was painted in a wide spectrum of colors – from black or ink blue, through every possible shade of blue and to pure white just above the horizon. By that time my right arm was completely out of commission, so I continued the flight using only my left hand. When I reached the point where I could no longer maintain positive control of the aircraft in the thin air, I decided to call it a day and headed back down. I ran a few speed tests during the descent and reported on their results back to Langenhagen. When I finally landed it was almost pitch black. The ground crew guys gave me a warm welcome, but I could tell they were all just itching to take a reading from the baro installed in the aircraft. The instrument recorded the altitude of 13 654 m."[3]

Having thoroughly tested the Fw 190 V 29/U! prototype, the staff at Erprobungsstelle Rechlin submitted a comprehensive test report:

"Summary of main findings:

1. Instability in pitch axis can be offset by use of trailing edge flaps.

2. The stalling characteristics are not benign, but can be accepted.

3. Poor stability in yaw axis. Aircraft demonstrates some tendency for uncommanded yaw in flight."[4]

Focke-Wulf replaced the lost Fw 190 V 33/U1 with the Fw 190 V 25, W.Nr. 110 025, which had been assembled at Sorau plant. The aircraft was first flown on December 15, 1944, but no archival records are available documenting its later use in the flight test program.

The fourth prototype of the Ta 152 H was the Fw 190 V 32/U1, W.Nr. 0057, GH+KV, which was delivered to Langenhagen on August 15, 1944. The aircraft was in fact a prototype of the Ta 152 C, which was to be modified with the wing removed from the damaged Ta 152 V 25. In its new configuration and fitted with a boosted Junkers Jumo 213 E-1 the aircraft made its first flight in late January 1945.

The fifth prototype example was the Fw 190 V 18/U2, W.Nr. 0040, CF+OY powered by the Jumo 213 E-1 engine equipped with the GM-1 and MW 50 systems. The aircraft featured wooden tail control surfaces and armor-plated engine cover. It was most likely flown for the first time on December 10, 1944. Less than

Focke-Wulf Ta 152 H high-altitude fighter

The Fw190 V 31, W.Nr. 0056, GH+KU was lost on May 28, 1943 when it crashed during a forced landing attempt near Kaltenweide.

two weeks later, probably on December 23, the machine was involved in a landing accident and suffered severe damage.

The first production model was the Ta 152 H-0, which was not equipped with integral wing fuel tanks or with MW 50 and GM-1 engine boost systems. The aircraft were assembled at Cottbus plant. The first production example, the Ta 152 H-0, W.Nr. 150 001, CW+CA, was flight tested on November 24, 1944 by Flugkapitän Hans Sander. Five days later, on November 29, 1944, Sander took off for a maiden flight in the second production fighter, the Ta 152 H-0, W.Nr. 150 002, CW+CB. The same pilot flown the Ta 152 H-0, W.Nr. 150 003, CW+CC on December 3, 1944. Eighteen more Ta 152 H-0s had been completed by the end of December 1944. It was during the same period that one of the aircraft, W.Nr. 150 025, was damaged during a landing mishap at Cottbus caused by the failure of the landing gear locking mechanism. The aircraft was subsequently repaired and delivered to III./JG 301 on January 27, 1945. In January twenty Ta 152 H-0s rolled off the assembly lines, followed by only three examples in February. The reason for this dramatic drop in production was unavailability of certain key subassemblies and complete disintegration of the supply system.

The cowling of the Junkers Jumo 213 with a characteristic air scoop (Fw 190 V 20).

The Focke-Wulf Fw 190 V 20, W.Nr. 0042, TI+IG was used as the prototype of the Ta 152 A.

In all likelihood the Cottbus plant manufactured 43 examples of the Ta 152 H.

On a beautiful, clear day of January 16, 1945 USAAF aircraft launched an attack on Neuhausen airfield used for flight testing of Focke-Wulf Ta 152 H fighters prior to delivery to frontline units. A U.S. force consisting of P-51s and P-38s pounded the airfield between 12.03 and 12.35 pm. The raiders came in from the west at 500 m and initially overflew the field without opening fire. Minutes later the U.S. fighters returned, this time at tree top level and approaching from the north-easterly and south-westerly directions. Some of the fighters began strafing the airfield flying as low as 3 meters off the deck. The Americans attacked in three waves targeting not only the aircraft parked on the airfield's perimeter, but also carefully camouflaged machines dispersed in the nearby woods. The base was very poorly protected against the airborne threat: all the Germans could muster against the U.S. fighters was a single 20 mm AA cannon and 10 twin MG 81 machine guns. It is therefore no wonder that the damage inflicted by the raid was very heavy indeed. No fewer than 14 Ta 152 Hs plus a single Fw 190 A were completely destroyed. Another Ta 152 H suffered 30 percent damage. A storage shed, housing various pieces of equipment, including aircraft batteries and charging units, went up in smoke.

The reason why so many Ta 152 H airframes had been lost in the raid was rather prosaic: the fighter's increased wing span meant the machines would not fit into dispersal pens, so the Fw 190 As were parked there instead. That explains why only one Fw 190 A was lost in the air raid.

By the time the full-scale production of the Ta 152 H was launched in November 1944 the Reich had begun to crumble under heavy pressure of Allied attacks. Incessant air raids forced Focke-Wulf to move their aircraft assembly lines to the eastern parts of the country, beyond the reach of the Allied bombers. However, the Soviets soon captured one of the Focke-Wulf assembly plants in Marienburg (Marlbork) in West Prussia. The Red Army sweeping through Wartheland, Oberschlesien and Niederschlesien broke up Focke-Wulf's supply chain and eliminated many smaller companies manufacturing all kinds of aircraft subassemblies.

Focke-Wulf struggled in the West as well. All the tooling necessary for mass production of the Ta 152 H was lost when the Allies captured a Focke-Wulf subcontractor in France. The plans to start the production of Ta 152 H in Italy, first drafted on May 9, 1944, had to be abandoned on July 24, 1944.

Despite the mounting problems the full-scale production of the fighter did begin in November 1944. The production ran into serious delays when snags were discovered in the cockpit pressurization system. It was not until December 11, 1944 that the first production example, the Ta 152 H-0, W.Nr. 150 003, was finally delivered to do Erprobungsstelle Rechlin for service trials.

Focke-Wulf Ta 152 H high-altitude fighter

The RLM 74/RLM 75 camouflage applied to the upper surfaces can be clearly seen in this shot of the Fw 190 V 20.

The Focke-Wulf Fw 190 V 21, W.Nr. 0043, TI+IH.

The pace of production process largely depended on the availability of raw materials and it often slowed down when substitutes of all sorts had to be used. There were constant problems with quality of various subassemblies manufactured at various locations. At some points the assembly lines came to a screeching halt when faulty welding was discovered in horizontal stabilizer main spar assemblies. The situation got even worse when the Soviets captured a plant in Posen (Poznań) responsible for final assembly of the Ta 152 H fuselage assemblies and wings. On February 22, 1945 Reichsmarschall Göring called a meeting to discuss the future of German aircraft production. The meeting resulted in limiting the number of Ta 152 versions considered for mass production. A decision was also made that the fighter would only be used in the fighter role, while modified Wf 190s would fill in the gap as fighter bombers.

In March 1945 pilot reports raised the issue of longitudinal stability problems of the Ta 152 H. The remedy was a recommendation to carry only 75 l of water-methanol mixture in the 140 l MW 50 tank. Additionally, the aircraft's received larger flight control surfaces and redesigned wing to fuselage sections.

On March 29, 1945 a team responsible for the Reich's armament production gathered to discuss the future of the Ta 152 program. Ultimately a decision was made to discontinue the aircraft's full-scale production in favor of the Focke-Wulf Fw 190 D powered by the Jumo 213 F engine. The decision was based solely on the basis of logistics (the loss of factories involved in the Ta 152 program) and did not in any way question the technological value of Kurt Tank's design.

According to the original plans, as many as 15 000 Ta 152s were to be manufactured by the end of 1946. In April 1945 a complete set of the Ta 152 technical documentation was sold to

An interesting shot of the Fw 190 V 21 showing detail of the engine exhaust manifold.

Japan. However, the war came to an end before the Japanese could make any use of the German technology.

Ta 152 in combat

The were plans to begin deliveries of the Ta 152s to Luftwaffe fighter units as early as the fall of 1944. However, the full-scale production of the fighter suffered delays when tooling for assembly lines in France was lost in the summer of 1944. New tooling sets had to be manufactured at Wocke-Wulf plant in Posen (Poznań). Therefore, the first three Ta 152 examples were not ready for delivery to the frontline units until October 1944.

The first Ta 152 H-0s assembled at Cottbus were delivered for service trials at Luftwaffe's test facility Erprobungsstelle Rechlin. The tests were designed to eliminate any faults in the design before the full-scale production was launched in earnest. The staff at Rechlin requested that no fewer than twelve Ta 152 H-0s be available for testing. The first example arrived on December 11, 1944. Before the year's end the remaining machines were delivered to Rechlin as well. All aircraft were assigned to an experimental unit designated Erprobungskommando Ta 152 (EK 152) under the command of Hauptmann Bruno Stelle. Stelle, a former member of I./JG 11, arrived in Rechlin on November 25, 1944. He was a highly accomplished combat pilot with 38 victories to his credit, including five heavy bomber kills. The Ta 152 test program at Rechlin was scheduled to be completed by April 1, 1945. There were plans to build up EK 152 to a strength of four squadrons, but ultimately the EK 152 designation was replaced in official documents with Stabsstaffel JG 301, which meant that the personnel of III./JG 301 had been involved in the test program.

On January 23, 1945 the Luftwaffe's High Command issued the following order: "With respect to the planned enlargement of the Ta 152 Experimental Unit (E-Kommando – author's note) the III./JG 301, as an experimental combat unit, shall receive the Ta 152 H-1 fighters. Additionally, the squadron shall continue to field its current types until otherwise instructed."[5]

Four days later, after the orders had been received by III./JG 301, a group of the unit's pilots was taken driven by a truck to Focke-Wulf factory at Neuhausen near Cottbus to pick up their new fighters and ferry them to Alteno airfield. When they arrived at Neuhausen all aircrews jumped up from their wooden benches when they saw 12 Tank Ta 152 H-0 and H-1 fighters lined up in three neat rows. At first they were greatly surprised: at first sight, those long-winged and long-nosed machines did not look like thoroughbred fighters. With rather mixed feelings, they pilots walked up to the parked machines to take a closer look and query the ground crews standing by the planes. After a thirty minute brief covering the key areas of the new design, the pilots jumped into the cockpits, fired up the engines and took of heading for Alteno. Fw. Willi Reschke from 9./JG 301 made some notes about his first flight in Tank's fighter: "The acceleration on take-off was tremendous – it just slammed me into the seat. The Ta was airborne after just several hundred meters of take-off roll. The climb rate was truly amazing. The long wings were very impressive and the flight controls felt fine. The cockpit was spacious enough and had good visibility. The landing speed was slightly lower than what I had been used to."[6]

The unit was supposed to receive a full complement of 35 Ta 152s, but because the Russians captured Focke-Wulf plant in Marienburg in West Prussia only 16 aircraft were ulti-

Ta 152 in combat

The Fw 190 V 68, W.Nr. 170 003, DU+JC was used in weapons trials of the Ta 152 B destroyer variant. The muzzle of an MK 103 30 mm cannon can be visible in the wing root.

mately delivered. The first batch included serials W.Nr. 150 001, 150 022, 150 025, 150 032 and 150 034 to 150 040.

Former members of III./JG 301 remember comfortable and spacious cockpit of the Ta 152. The canopy, almost a perfect bubble type, provided excellent visibility in all directions. Huge amounts of power delivered by Jumo 231 E could be felt as soon as the aircraft began its take-off roll. Instant acceleration pushed the pilot into his seat and the machine easily broke ground at 210 km/h. Gear and flap retraction was almost a non-event in the Ta 152, unlike the Fw 190 which had a pronounced sinking tendency once the flaps had been raised. Tank's fighter also featured a huge propeller producing a lot of forward thrust thanks to its massive blades with the chord of 60 cm.

The fighter could climb at 17.5 m/s up to 5 000 m. It required just twelve minutes to reach the altitude of 10 000 m, which produced an average climb rate of 14.5 m/s. During tests of one of the Ta 152 H-0s the three-stage supercharger worked flawlessly, although later on, in actual combat applications, the unit's third stage would occasionally fail to kick in.

The Ta 152 responded very well to control inputs up to the altitude of 10 000 m. In that regard it compared very favorably to the Fw 190 A-8 which was very unstable at such high altitudes. It was not until the fighter climbed to 12 800 meters that first signs of degraded control became visible.

The first mock engagements that pitted the new fighter against the unit's standard Fw 190 A-8s showed the Tank's superiority in classic dog fights. The new fighter's advantage was especially pronounced at altitudes between 6 000 and 8 000 m. Many of the unit's pilots commented that the aircraft could practically turn on a dime. By mid March 1945 all of the flight crews of III./JG 301 had an opportunity to log time in the Ta 152. The unit's logs show no fewer than 120 Ta 152 sorties totaling 40 hours that had been flown by February 14, 1945.

A that time III./JG 301 was commanded by Maj. Guth, with Lt. Schröder serving as adjutant and Hptm. Hölzer holding the post of technical officer. On February 14, 1945 Hölzer was transferred to I./JG 301 and was replaced by Oblt. Schallenberg from II./JG 301.

On February 1, 1945 the squadron lost its first Ta 152 H, W.Nr. 150 037. Uffz. Hermann Dürr from 12./JG 301 was on a training sortie when the aircraft entered a flat spin and

The Focke-Wulf Ta 152 V 6, W.Nr. 110 006, VH+EY was the first prototype of the Ta 152 C. The fighter first flew on December 12, 1944.

crashed just one kilometer east of the filled killing the pilot. Another aircraft, W.Nr. 150 022 suffered damage in a landing mishap, but it was quickly repaired and returned to service. On average, 75 percent of the Ta 152 Hs were ready to fight at any given time. The situation deteriorated briefly in early February 1945 when the unit received a batch of contaminated fuel, which damaged fuel injectors in Jumo 213 engines. At that stage only 30 percent of the unit's Ta 152 Hs were airworthy. Thanks to experienced and highly trained ground personnel, commanded by Hptm. Hölzer, all faults were quickly rectified.

Located in a close proximity to the front, Alteno airfield was home to several fighter and ground attack units. To provide a safer and quieter environment for trials of the Ta 152 H, a decision was made to move III./JG 301 to Alperstedt near Erfurt. Eventually, the unit was transferred to Sachau instead of Alperstedt.

At the same time Hptm. Gerhard Posselmann became the new CO of I./JG 301. His post as the CO of 9. Staffel was given to Oblt. Hermann Stahl, who began his combat career with 12./JG 51.

By the early days of February 1945 Germany was losing the war on all fronts. This led to a desperate decision to use all available assets from Luftwaffe flight test centers for combat operations. To that end Gefechtsverband Kommando der Erprobung (K.d.E), or special operational experimental group, was established at Rechlinunder the command of Obst. Petersen. The unit was equipped with a variety of types, including Bf 109, Me 262, Fw 190, Ar 234 and eight examples of the Tank Ta 152 H (as of February 9, 1945). Tank fighters were incorpo-

Air intake of the DB 603 EC.

The Ta 152 V 6 was armed with a pair of fuselage mounted MG 151/20 20 mm cannons and two additional MG 151/20s in the wing roots.

On January 8, 1945 the Focke-Wulf Ta 152 V 7, W.Nr. 110 007, CI+XM made its first flight powered by the Daimler-Benz DB 603 EC.

Ta 152 in combat

Cowling of the Daimler-Benz DB 603 EC as installed on the Ta 152 V 7.

The Focke-Wulf Ta 152 V 7 was equipped with the MW 50 water-methanol injection system and had the wing area of 19.50 m².

rated into an independent fighter squadron designated Jagdstaffel Ta 152 based at Roggentin airfield and commanded by Hptm. Bruno Stolle. By February 4, 1945 the unit had been renamed to "Jagdstaffel Roggentin". There were plans to use the unit's fighters on the Eastern Front, but there are no archival records supporting that thesis. What is known and documented is that the unit fielded the following Ta 152 aircraft: Ta 152 H W.Nr. 150 003 (CW+CC), 10 006 (CW+CF), 150 008, 150 009 (CW+CI), 150 010 (CW+CJ), 150 011 and Ta 152 C V8, W.Nr. 110 008 (GW+QA).

At around the same time the Focke-Wulf prepared a report summarizing the results of the Ta 152 H tests while in service with III./JG 301. "The opinion of the members of III./JG 301 about the Ta 152 H-0 surpassed anything else that had been said about any other new weapons system introduced into operational service with the Luftwaffe. In particular, good turning performance had been praised. The number of faults reported during the tests appears to be much below the average expected for a brand new weapons system. Moreover, most of them (with the exception of issues with hydraulic landing gear extension and retraction system) cannot be classified as serious fault that could preclude the immediate deployment of the aircraft.

It is also noteworthy that while rectification of various faults was necessary to maintain combat readiness of the unit, all the required work had been performed at the squadron level. It is expected that lessons learned will be applied in manufacturing of subsequent machines, especially that the number of issues involved is not large indeed. While communicating with their superiors, the squadron members did not report each individual fault, but rather presented a general summary of positive char-

The Focke-Wulf Ta 152 V 7 photographed in the spring of 1945 after installation of the DB 603 LA powerplant.

An interesting shot of the Ta 152 V 7 parked at Langenhagen.

acteristics of the machine and assured the command that all faults would be dealt with in close cooperation with the manufacturer.

a) Flight characteristics

Compared to the Fw 190 A-8 the Ta 152 H-0 is capable of performing tighter turns without dropping the nose. The tendency becomes visible only at significantly slower speeds. Even when the aircraft departed controlled flight and went into a spin, it was easily recoverable by applying forward pressure on the stick. Spin recovery usually took some 500 to 600 m of altitude. During a mock fight between an A-8 with a seasoned pilot at the controls and the H-0 flown by a pilot making his second flight in the type, the A-8 was quickly outmaneuvered. All the above characteristics had been tested close to the ground or at altitudes of up to 3 000 m."[7]

One of the training sorties flown from Sachau claimed another Ta 152 H assigned to III./JG 301. The mishap pilot was Ofhr. Jonny Wiegeshoff, who perished in the crash. Wiegeshoff was recovering to Sachau when he decided to make a low pass over the field. The aircraft came in low and looked very slow to observers on the ground – almost as if some invisible force was holding it back. Reaching the end of the field the pilot pitched up, but the airspeed was too low to allow a climbing left turn. The aircraft stalled and went straight down into a group of trees at the edge of the airfield.

The accident was hard to explain. Members of the squadron who witnessed the crash were scratching their heads trying to understand why the aircraft did not have sufficient flying speed. While Oberfähnrich Wiegeshoff might not have been one of the most experienced Luftwaffe pilots, he was no rookie, either. Prior to join-

The same aircraft pictured in front of one of the hangars.

Ta 152 in combat

A close-up showing the air scoop and the wing root port of the MG 151/20 (Ta 152 V 7).

Cowling of the DB 603 LA as installed on the Ta 152 V 7.

ing the squadron in September 1944 he had done well in combat, shooting down four or five enemy aircraft. He had also received the Iron Cross 1st Class. Wiegeshoff was buried with full military honors ceremony at a cemetery in Gardelegen.

On February 25, 1945 I., II. and III./JG 301 were scrambled to intercept a USAAF raid on railroad hubs in Salzwedel, Wittenberg and Stendal. A force of ten Ta 152 H-0/H-1s and a dozen or so Fw 190 A-8/A-9s launched from Sachau and headed towards Braunschweig before turning north. A short time later the squadron's CO, Maj. Guth, reported engine failure and aborted the mission. To protect the CO from ever present Mustang threat, Uffz. Blum and Fw. Reschke decided to escort the major back to base. Less than an hour later all three aircraft landed safely at Sachau.

The CO's abort stirred some confusion among the squadron's pilots, although that was by no means the reason why they failed to make contact with the enemy. Later that night the mess hall was awfully quiet. That was not how everybody imagined the Ta 152's combat debut.

On March 2, 1945 1 232 USAAF heavy bombers launched from their bases in England accompanied by 774 P-47 and P-51 escort fighters. The bomber's targets were chemical plants in Böhlen and Chemnitz and industrial estates around Magdeburg. Once again all airworthy aircraft from JG 301 were scrambled to intercept the inbound raid. III./JG 301 sent up twelve Ta 152 H-0/H-1s and the same number of Fw 190 A-8/A-9s. The Tanks were tasked with providing top cover for the entire Geschwader and engaging enemy fighters to allow the Fw 190 As to attack the bombers. The Ta 152 H pilots, led by Oblt. Stahl, quickly took up position above the Fw 190s. The other machines from JG 301 joined up soon, including Bf 109 G-10s from IV./JG 301. Arrival of additional guns was music to the ears of the Tank pilots. Their joy quickly turned to sheer terror when they realized the Bf 109s began to fire at them. The leader of the Ta 152 formation immediately broke radio silence and radioed a command to the incoming Messerschmitts: "Continue your climb, maintain formation!". Despite the radio call, the Messerschmitt pilots pressed on their attacks. The Ta 152 crews had no option but to break up the formation and run for their lives, which effectively ended their mission. The Bf 109 pilots would soon pay a hefty price for their poor aircraft recognition skills. After their brief encounter with the Ta 152s the scattered Messerschmitt formation came under a sudden attack by a large force of USAAF Mustangs. The crews from IV./JG 301, mostly Eastern Front veterans with little or no experience in fighting against the Americans, suffered horrendous losses. To their obvious disadvantage almost all of the German fliers were former bomber pilots from III./KG 1 "Hindenburg". In a clash that lasted just minutes the U.S. fighters shot down no fewer than thirteen Bf 109s killing eight Luftwaffe pilots and wounding eight more. The squadron would never recover from that fatal blow. In early April 1945 the surviving members of the unit were assigned to three remaining JG 301 squadrons.

The losses of I./JG 301 included three aircraft, one pilot killed in action and two more listed as missing. II./JG 301 lost nine aircraft. Eight aircrews were killed and one suffered serious wounds. The operation of March 2, 1945 was the last large-scale combat mission of JG 301.

It soon turned out that III./JG 301 would not receive new Ta 152 to replace the machines lost in combat. Therefore, on March 13, 1945 the unit's CO ordered all serviceable aircraft to be assigned to the HQ flight. Additionally, four new pilots joined the squadron: Fw. Willi Reschke (9. Staffel), Uffz. Christoph Blum (9. Staffel), Ofw. Sepp Sattler (10. Staffel) and Ofw. Josef Keil (10 Staffel). On the same day Fw. Willi Reschke from Stab III./JG 301 ferried the Ta 152 H-1 "black 13" from Sachau to Stendal. where the Geschwader commander presented him with the German Cross in Gold (*Deutsches Kreuz in Gold*). At the same time the II./JG 301 base at Stendal was being inspected by the General der Jagdflieger Gen.Lt. Dietrich Pelz, who quickly jumped at the opportunity to go for a quick hop in Reschke's "black 13".

Several days later Fw. Willi Reschke launched from Stendal to intercept a British Mosquito. The nearby Freya and Würzburg stations quickly vectored the German fighter to its target and soon the two aircraft merged over Genthin. The RAF crew were on their return leg back to base flying at 9 000 m. Reschke was several hundred meters below the British machine, so he firewalled the throttle and continued the climb, maneuvering to position his fighter behind the Mosquito's tail. Less than a minute later he was in a perfect firing position with the Mosquito filling up his Revi gun sight. Reschke made a quick radio call and prepared to commence the attack. When he was about to squeeze the trigger, his Ta 152 shuddered and suddenly lost power. Reschke quickly realized that the supercharger's third stage had just failed. The British aircraft quickly disappeared into the distance, while Reschke had no choice but to abort the mission and return to base. Mechanical malfunctions were not rare, but the Luftwaffe ground crews usually dealt with them quickly and efficiently. What really hurt the unit

Details of the aft fuselage section and tail wheel assembly of the Ta 152 V 7.

The Focke-Wulf Fw 190 V 30/U1, W.Nr. 0050, GH+KT made its maiden flight on August 6, 1944.

Ta 152 in combat

This head-on shot of the Fw 190 V 30/U 1 offers a good view of the new, longer wing.

A close-up of engine cowling of the Ta 152 V 7.

was the lack new aircraft to compensate for combat attrition. It was not until April 8, 1945 that a rumor began to circulate around Standal airfield that two brand new Ta 152s were awaiting delivery at Erfurt-Nord. The rumor soon proved to be true and two pilots (Ofw. Reschke and Fw. Blum) were sent to Erfurt to collect the priceless fighters. Reschke later described the experience: "We were very much aware of the constant threat posed by enemy fighters roaming the skies over Germany, so we flew to Erfurt at tree top level to avoid any trouble. After a safe landing we taxied our Ar 96 straight into a hangar. The two Ta 152s were parked just outside and we quickly took stock of the machines. Both aircraft were fueled and carried a full complement of weapons, although the ammunition magazines were empty. Ads we taxied out in our unarmed fighters, air raid sirens began to wail announcing the arrival of American fighter bombers clearing the way for enemy armored spearheads. Although we were flying really fast machines, we both knew that we really couldn't put up a fight with not a single round of ammunition in our guns. Fortunately we managed to avoid trouble and landed safely at Stendal. Now the Geschwaderstab had two brand new Ta 152 H-1s on its strength."[8]

At around the same time Uffz. Herber Kordas from III./JG 301 based at Sachau received a radio message that 18 Ta 152 were ready for immediate collection at Celle airfield. When the excited squadron aircrews arrived at Celle they could not believe what they saw: all Ta 152s had damaged tail wheel assemblies rendering the fighters unairworthy.

By April 10,1945 the rumble of big artillery pieces could be clearly heard at all JG 301 bases. The frontlines were drawing closer and closer. During the night of April 10/11, 1945 the ground personnel of Geschwaderstab and II./JG 301 set off to a new base at Neustadt-Glewe near Ludwigslust in Mecklenburg. All airworthy fighters departed the following morning taking off literarily in front of the U.S. tanks which had rolled to within yards of the airfield's perimeter. The remaining JG 301 units vacated their bases over the next few days. On April 18 I. and III./JG 301 arrived at their new airfield at Hagenow near Schwerin, not far from Ludwigslust. The airbase at Neustadt-Glewe was located in a heavily forested area, which was ideal for concealment of the aircraft. Standing at the edge of the woods were wooden huts serving as living quarters and the unit's command post. Small metal hangars were located at the north-western edge of the field. The base was well protected against airborne threats with twin 20 mm cannon batteries positioned around the perimeter.

No sooner did the HQ flight and II./JG 301 arrive at Neustadt-Glewe than the crews were ordered to attack U.S. mechanized units that had just taken their former base at Stendal. Over Stendal Ta 152s from the HQ flight provided top cover for their mates from II./JG 301. At some point the Ta 152 pilots spotted a formation of P-47s, but the Americans refused to engage and quickly departed the area. One of the escaping Thunderbolts was hit by Ofw. Jupp Keil flying a Ta 152 H.

Life was not easy for Ta 152 crews operating from Neustadt-Glewe. Allied fighters main-

This shot of the Fw 190 V 30/U1 shows the camouflage pattern on the upper surfaces to good advantage. On August 23, 1944 the aircraft was destroyed in a landing crash which claimed the life of its pilot, Alfred Thomas.

tained almost constant presence over the base and it was the task of the HQ flight to perform fighter sweeps before any operations could be launched from the field. The procedure was the same prior to recovery of the squadron's fighters after an operational sortie. In order to improve the Stabgeschwader's odds in performing those critical tasks, two very experienced pilots were assigned to the flight. One of them was Ofw. Walter Loos who had formerly flown as a wingman of the CO of JG 300, Obst. Walter Dahl. The other pilot was the former CO of 9./JG 301 Oblt. Hermann Stahl. Availability of additional aircrews meant that the Stabgeschwader could now launch two Ta 152 H sections simultaneously.

The HQ flight did not suffer a single combat loss for the remainder of the war, a testament not only to the aircrew's skill and experience but also to the outstanding characteristics of their mounts. Moreover, despite heavy pressure

Another close-up photograph of the Ta 152 V 7 showing details of the cockpit and the wing to fuselage area.

The Focke-Wulf Fw 190 V 32/U1, W.Nr. 0057, GH+KV equipped with a four-bladed propeller.

Ta 152 in combat

The third production example of the Focke-Wulf Ta 152 H-0, W.Nr. 150 003, CW+CC. Hans Sander was at the controls for the fighter's maiden flight on December 3, 1944.

The Ta 152 H-0, W.Nr. 150 003 at Focke-Wulf factory airfield at Cottbus. The aircraft carries a 300 l drop tank on the centerline station.

from Allied fighters, only one of the squadron's aircraft (from II./JG 301) was shot down while recovering to Neustadt-Glewe.

Ta 152s took off and landed under the protective umbrella provided by the field's strong AAA defenses. However, the fighter's characteristics were so good that it was ready to fight just minutes after take-off, as soon as the pilot cleaned up the landing gear and flaps. On landing, the high lift devices and wide-track landing gear provided for a quick exit from the runway and taxi to the dispersal area.

However, things did not go smoothly all the time. Fw. Blum from Stabschwarm/JG 301 had a close call on April 13, 1945 as he was coming in to land after another combat sortie. For some reason the German pilot did not notice a Spitfire that took up position just behind his tail. For quite a while both aircraft flew in a perfect trail formation, which looked to the German AAA crews like a pair of Luftwaffe fighters making their final approach to land. It was not until both machines flew over the runway threshold that the gunners understood their mistake and opened fire shooting off the tail of the British fighter. The Spitfire snapped into a half-roll and crashed within the airfield's perimeter.

On the following day, despite poor weather conditions, the crews of JG 301 flew a low-level attack sortie against Soviet positions along the

40

Ta 152 in combat

The same aircraft as seen from behind and from the right. Notice the long wings typical for the H models.

This interesting shot of the Ta 152 H-0, W.Nr. 150 003 shows camouflage pattern on the aircraft's upper surfaces.

Oder River, north of Berlin. Six Ta 152 H fighters from Geschwaderstab which provided top cover for the attack did not make contact with the enemy.

Later that day Oblt. Auffammer, Ofw. Sattler and Ofw. Reschke launched in their Ta 152s to intercept a pair of Hawker Tempests flying along the Ludigslust-Schwerin railroad line. As the German fighters were approaching their targets, the aircraft flown by . Sepp Sattler suddenly departed controlled flight, went straight down and exploded upon impact with the ground. The remaining two pilots pressed on their attack: "The Tempest had a reputation for being a very fast fighter. The British often used it successfully against the V1s. However, in that particular encounter speed didn't matter that much. We were close to the ground and it was maneuverability that made the difference. When I was setting up for the attack the Englishman had just begun a pull-up from a strafing pass. I quickly attacked him in a tight, left-hand turn.

A wild dog fight began. I kept closing in on the Tempest at heights almost never exceeding 50 m. I never once felt that my aircraft was flying at the edge of its performance envelope. To avoid my murderous fire the Tempest pilot had to perform wild turns and twists, but my Ta 152 continued to close the gap between us. Eventually the Tempest began to drop its wing in a turn, which clearly showed it couldn't turn any harder. I fired a burst which hit his aft fuselage and tail section. The Tempest pilot countered with a right-hand turn, which in fact was even better for me. He was now in a trap. I squeezed the triggers again, but the guns remained silent. I tried re-cocking them, but that didn't help either. Today I can't recall the exact combination of curses that shot out from my mouth at that time. Luckily, the Tempest pilot wasn't aware of my predicament. Having been shot once he continued his crazy dance while I tried to stay right behind him. Then suddenly I saw vapor trails behind his wings as the Tempest dropped the left wing and went straight down into a forest below. The entire fight took place just 10 m over the trees and rooftops, a very unusual dogfight indeed. My Ta 152 performed flawlessly and responded extremely well to even slightest control inputs.

Since the fight took place just a few kilometers from our base, in the afternoon we went to

Inline Junkers Jumo 213 E-1 powered Focke-Wulf Ta 152 H fighters.

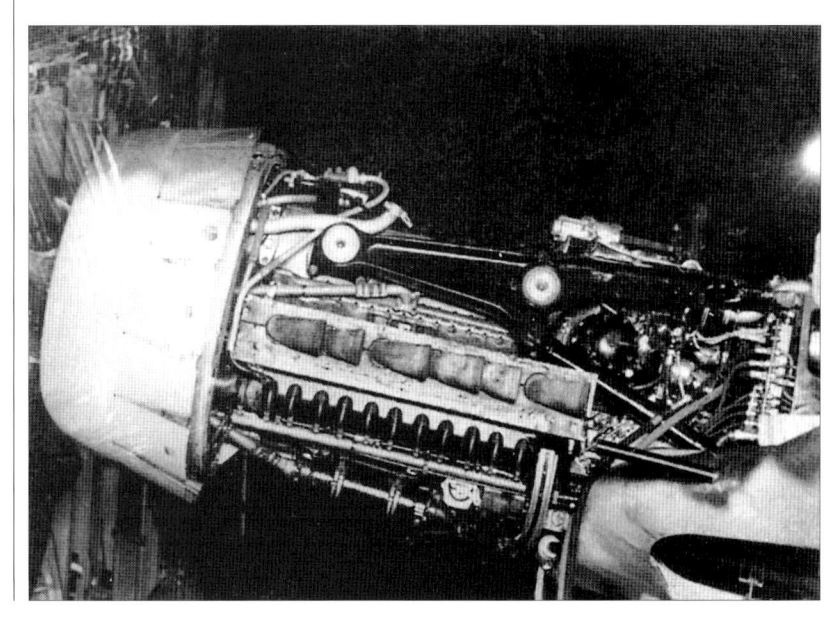

Focke-Wulf Ta 152 — 41

Ta 152 in combat

Inline Junkers Jumo 213 E-1 powered Focke-Wulf Ta 152 H fighters.

Cockpit of the Ta 152 H-0. The gauges on the main instrument panel are, from left to right, turn and bank indicator, VSI, directional gyro, boost pressure indicator and fuel flow indicator.

inspect the Tempest crash site. We soon found out that the British aircraft crashed just 500 m from Ofw. Sattler's Ta 152. The trees cushioned the impact and it looked as if the Tempest had almost made a successful crash landing. The fighter's fuselage and tail were badly shot up and the pilot's body was still strapped in the cockpit. We later established the Tempest was flown by a New Zealander Warrant Officer O. J. Mitchell from the RAF's No. 486 Squadron."[9]

Oblt. Auffhammer engaged the other Tempest and quickly got on his tail. However, the British pilot, maneuvering just meters off the ground and using every terrain feature to his advantage, managed to evade the attack and escaped to the west.

The technical officer of JG 301, Hptm. Roderich Cescotti witnessed the fight from the ground: "During my tenure as the TO of JG 301 I had an opportunity to fly the Ta 152 H-0 and H-1. On April 4 and 7, 1945 I made five take-offs and landing logging about one hour at the controls (...). Thanks to the three-stage supercharger the Jumo 213 E delivered its full power at 10 500 m. The Ta 152 with its long wing remained fully controllable up to some 14 000 m, which in those times was quite remarkable for a stock fighter. The long, slender wing also made the aircraft very agile at low altitudes and gave it a decisive edge over the Tempest. One of the encounters that clearly demonstrated that point took place right over our base at Neustadt-Glewe.

Ta 152 H-1s from Geschwaderführungskette were scrambled to intercept an inbound formation of four Tempests. Soon after take-off three Ta 152s engaged the British and a series of dogfights ensued between the ground level and some 4 000 meters. From the very beginning the Tempest pilots found it difficult to capitalize on their 4 v 3 advantage. The fourth Ta 152 experienced some problems during engine start-up and its pilot, Ofw. Sepp Sattler took off several minutes after the section led by Obstl. Fritz Auffhammer. Sattler quickly climbed above the aircraft engaged in the fight and then dived on the enemy aircraft with the sun behind his back. He shot down one of the Tempests before plunging into the ground from around 2 000 meters without any visible signs of attempted recovery.

(...) Another Ta 152, flown by Ofw. Willi Reschke was chasing a Tempest at tree-top heights. At some point, when Reschke was in a perfect firing position, his guns jammed. The Tempest continued to fly a series of very violent evasive maneuvers until its pilot lost control and impacted the ground. The odds were now stacked up 3:2 in Ta 152 favor. The remaining two Tempests opted to disengage and run for their lives.

Our CO chased one of them at medium to high altitudes, but despite his huge combat experience could not get a bead on the Englishman. As it later turned out his supercharger was set for maximum performance at low altitudes, which greatly degraded engine operation at higher levels. The culprit was quickly identified as the malfunctioning automatic supercharger controller. Despite this disadvantage the Ta 152 in the hands of Obstl. Auffhammer was still evenly matched with the Tempest."[10]

On April 20, 1945, the Führer's birthday, Ofw. Walter Loos and Ofw. Willi Reschke z Geschwaderstab/JG 301 received the Knight's Crosses for their accomplishments in defense of the Reich.

On April 21, 1945 Ta 152 H fighters launched from their base at Neustadt-Glewe to provide top cover for aircraft from II./JG 301 tasked with supporting ground units engaging Soviet troops along the Oder River, south of Berlin. Initially it was all quiet both in the air and down on the ground. However, when

Ta 152 in combat

they approached the area between Storkow and Beeskow the Luftwaffe formation was caught in murderous AAA fire. The German pilots, having problems establishing the exact location of the frontline, attacked the Soviet AAA positions. As the Focke-Wulfs were about to turn back home, several Yak-9 fighters arrived on the scene. Ofw. Jupp Keil, flying a Ta 152 H, engaged the Yaks and shot down two of them in short order.

April 24, 1945 was the last time that all squadrons of JG 301 operated together as a cohesive unit. Their task was a bombing and strafing attack against Soviet positions near Zossen, just east of Berlin. At 0800 hours the Ta 152 H fighters launched from Neustadt-Glewe, followed several minutes later by Fw 190s from II./JG 301. At the same time the fighters from I. and III./JG 301 were taking off from Hagenow. The entire formation had a strength of just one full squadron – most of the flights consisted of just individual *schwarms*.

The HQ flight, consisting of a pair and a section of Ta 152s, was the first element to become airborne. As usual, the Ta 152s provided airborne protection for aircraft from II./JG 301. At the controls of the Tanks were Oblt. Stahl and Ofw. Reschke, followed by Ofw. Loos, Ofw. Keil and Fw. Blum. The low cloud ceilings of 1 500 m made it practically impossible to provide proper cover for the Fw 190s from II./JG 301. Under those conditions the pair of Ta 152s took up position on the left side of the formation, while the three aircraft section remained on the right side. The transit to the target area was uneventful. Nobody knew the exact location of the frontlines, so the pilots had to rely on enemy AAA fire to show them the way. By than the Luftwaffe crews had learned that red tracers always indicated Soviet AAA, as opposed to yellow smoke produced by German rounds.

The weather was over the target area was not much better than it had been en-route, so setting up a coordinated attack of 70 aircraft that JG 301 had mustered that day was not an easy task. It was very difficult to distinguish between enemy and friendly positions among the lakes and woodlands around Zossen. Each pilot would have to make his own decisions and select targets to the best of his abilities. Nobody knew at the time if the bombs that JG 301 dropped actually hit anything, but the strafing passes were indeed successful, plus there were no Soviet fighters in the area to interrupt the attack runs.

In the mission brief the Ta 152 crews had been given an additional task: perform post attack reconnaissance of the area around Zossen. In order to establish the location of frontlines

Another photograph of the Ta 152 H-0 cockpit. Some of the controls located on the left console include FuG 16 ZY tuning panel, horizontal stabilizer indicator, stabilizer trim control and throttle lever.

The Focke-Wulf Ta 152 H-0, W.Nr. 150 005, CW+CE photographed at Focke-Wulf' Cottbus plant during calibration of flight instruments.

Ta 152 in combat

Focke-Wulf Ta 152 Hs in service with III./JG 301 photographed at Alteno near Luckau in February 1945. The aircraft in the background is "yellow 1" from 7. Staffel. Notice the characteristic Reich Defense tail band.

Ofw. Josef Keil from JG 301 photographed in January 1945 at Sachau. Keil was credited with five air-to-air kills at the controls of the Ta 152 H.

around Berlin the three-ship section would head south of the capital, while a pair of Ta 152s would follow the route plotted to the north of the city. After the last Geschwader machines had finished their air-to-ground work, the HQ flight, as had been previously agreed, split up into two sections and followed their pre-assigned routes. Ofw. Reschke remembers: "Oblt. Stahl and myself flew past the radio towers at Königs-Wusterhausen setting up on course that would take us just east of Berlin before turning towards Neustadt-Glewe. As soon as we reached the lakes between Königs-Wusterhausen and Erkner we saw red tracers coming up towards us. It was a clear sign that the Russians were now very close to Berlin. We were flying in a loose formation some 200 meters apart trying to remain clear of the overcast at 1 500 m. We would occasionally lose visual contact with each other flying through some scattered clouds below the main cloud ceiling. In poor visibility I suddenly spotted a pair of Soviet fighters approaching from the right. I immediately realized that the Soviets, coming in from behind and from the right, were maneuvering to attack Oblt. Stahl. I called the threat over the radio and turned towards the enemy fighters. I was really surprised to see Stahl continue straight and level, taking no evasive action. The only thing he did was descend slightly. Despite my frantic radio calls to pull up into the clouds and seemingly oblivious to red tracers zooming past his aircraft, Stahl continued straight as an arrow.

In the meantime, as I had just got on the tail of one of the Yak-9s, I saw tracer rounds whizzing past my cockpit. Trying to help out Oblt. Stahl I forgot to look after myself and now I was in some serious trouble. I immediately pitched up into a left-hand climbing turn to shake off the Russian sitting on my tail. I then realized that I was dealing with a whole section of Yaks chasing me allover the sky. Having followed Stahl for quite a while I was now quite low, so the Russians had to problems keeping up with me in that first turn. It was my first encounter with the Soviets and I knew precious little about their combat tactics. All I knew was that I could always try and seek refuge in the clouds. The Russians maintained tight formation which made it difficult for me to turn as hard as I would have wanted to. At some point, however, I realized I was no longer in front of them, but behind them. The Ta 152 once again proved its excellent turning capability. The Russian formation did not scatter until their number 4 went down under a volley of bullets from my guns. Now each of the remaining Soviet pilots was trying to get a piece of me. In truth, only one of them showed some fighting spirit. The other two Yaks quickly disengaged and left the area. The lone Soviet fighter, probably flown by the commander of that small fighting outfit, was now on his own trying to slug it out with a far superior Ta 152. Within minutes his Yak was riddled with bullets and the Russian had to run for his life trailing black smoke. The engagement was fought just north of Erkner, along the line extending towards Neuenhagen.

During the fight I lost contact with Oblt. Stahl, so I tried to raise him on the radio. Looking down at a multitude of fires burning around Berlin I wasn't sure if one of them could be Stahl's aircraft.

The entire Geschwader was still airborne at that time with our Ta 152 three-ship section engaging Soviet fighters south of Berlin. There was a lot of chatter on the frequency, which made it so much more difficult to get Stahl on the radio. I could only hope he was still in one piece and that he would make it safely back to the base.

At 0915 my Ta 152 H-1, W.Nr. 150 168, "green 9" touched down at Neustadt-Glewe airfield. I didn't know it at that time but it was my last combat sortie and the last dogfight of the war.

In the final weeks of the war the Ta 152 was my life insurance policy: without its excellent performance my chances of survival would have been a lot slimmer."[11]

Oblt. Hermann Stahl did not return from the combat sortie and was listed as missing in action. All post-war attempts to solve the mystery of his disappearance failed and to this day his fate remains unknown. During the battles over Berlin on April 24, 1945 the Geschwaderstab Ta 152s shot down four Soviet Yak-9s. A pair of Yaks were dispatched by Ofw. Reschke over Erkner, while the other two fell victim to Ofw. Walter Loos just south of Berlin. JG 301 launched its final combat sorties of the war on April 30, 1945. The unit's Fw 190s attacked Russian positions around Berlin, while the high-flying Ta 152 H fighters engaged a formation of Yaks. Ofw. Walter Loos bagged a single Russian fighter, while Uffz. Willi Greiner from 12./JG 301 flying an Fw 190 A-9 downed another one. Those were the last kills obtained by JG 301 in World War II.

Immediately after the last sorties, the personnel of Stabschwarm and II./JG 301 was ordered to travel by road to Leck airfield in Schleswig-Holstein. The aircraft were to remain at Neustadt-Glewe, where they would be taken over by JG 11.

It is difficult to establish the actual number of kills achieved by Ta 152 H pilots. It was certainly not lower than 13, with no fewer than five scored by Josef Keil. Willy Reschke and Walter Loos were each credited with four air-to-air victories. Four Ta 152 H were lost in combat operations, including two aircraft that went missing during a ferry flight to Leck in the final days of the war.

Post-war fate of the Ta 152

After the war the Allies could not wait to get their hands on German aircraft designs which had either entered service with the Luftwaffe in the final stages of the war, or were still sitting

General der Jagdflieger Gen. Maj. Dietrich Pelz (in the middle) inspecting Stendal airfield on March 14, 1945. Standing to his left is the CO of JG 301 Obstlt. Fritz Auffhammer. The CO of II./JG 301, Hptm. Herbert Nölter, is standing to the right. Visible in the background is part of the fuselage of the Ta 152 H-0, W.Nr. 150 007, "black 3", which was flown by Ofw. Willi Reschke.

Gen. Maj. Dietrich Pelz donning a flight suit is getting ready for a hop in the Ta 152 H-0, W.Nr. 150 007. Standing in the middle is Obstlt. Auffhammer, while Hptm. Nölter (on the right) is looking on.

Gen. Maj. Pelz photographed by the canopy of the Ta 152 H-0. The massive frame indicates the windshield was manufactured using 70 mm armored glass.

Post-war fate of the Ta 152

Gen. Maj. Pelz in the cockpit of the Ta 152 H-0. The fuel triangle is just visible in the right hand corner.

The CO of II./JG 301, Hptm. Nölter addresses his men at Stendal on March 15, 1945. The aircraft in the background, on the right hand side, is a Ta 152 H.

Ofw. Sepp Sattler from Stab JG 301 died at the controls of a Ta 152 H on April 14, 1945.

in factories and various research facilities. The Ta 152 was not high on the Allied shopping list, since by that time they had already had their own high-performance piston-powered fighters. It was the jets that they wanted most.

Although the service career of the Ta 152 ended when Nazi Germany formally surrendered on May 8, 1945, the Allied troops captured several airworthy examples of the fighter. At Erfurt-Nord airfield the Americans found the Ta 152 H-1, W.Nr. 150 167, which was supposed to be converted into a Ta 152 H-10 reconnaissance variant. The technical report A-377 describes the aircraft as fully airworthy. The fighter was never transported back to the U.S. and was later scrapped along with Fw 190 D-9s that used to belong to JG 301.

The airframe that did make it back to the USA was the Focke-Wulf Ta 152 H-0, W.Nr. 150 010, CW+CJ captured at Tirstrup airfield in Denmark. Initially the British took charge of the aircraft, but it was later handed over to Americans at Aalborg. Captain Fred McIntosh of "Watson's Whizzers" (a dedicated unit responsible for ferrying captured German aircraft) flew the fighter to Melun-Villaroche in France. Later it was delivered to the port city of Cherbourg and loaded onto HMS Reaper for a journey across the Atlantic. When the fighter arrived at Newark, New Jersey it received the FE-112 registration (FE standing for "Foreign Evaluation") before ending up at Freeman Field, Indiana where it joined other ex-Luftwaffe machines. At least on one occasion the aircraft is known to have been at Wright Field base in Ohio. Currently the aircraft resides at National Air and Space Museum awaiting restoration.

Another Ta 152 ended up in the United Kingdom. The Focke-Wulf Ta 152 H-1, W.Nr. 150 168, "green 9" (the aircraft in which Willi Reschke scored his two kills on April 24) was taken apart at Schleswig airfield and airlifted to Britain aboard an Arado Ar 232 B transport. The fighter arrived at Farnborough on August 3, 1945, where it was subsequently flight tested at Royal Aircraft Establishment. On August 18, 1945 the famous British test pilot Eric Brown ferried the fighter from Farnborough to Brize Norton: "I cannot recall that, after re-assembly, it was put through any specific flight testing other than that I was instructed to perform while flying it from Farnborough to Brize Norton for storage during the summer of 1945.

The original radial-engined Fw 190 had been, in my view, an aerodynamic beauty oozing lethality, but it struck me on first seeing the Ta 152H-1 standing outside Farnborough's famous ‚A' shed in the company of the latest Allied fighters – the Tempest V, the Mustang III, the Spitfire 21 and the Martin-Baker M.B.5 – that Tank's design had lost much of its aesthetic appeal over the intervening years. If now less curvaceous, it still exuded efficiency, however, and I had little doubt that it was capable of doing all that the Germans claimed for it.

High performance at all altitudes was ensured by its 18.71 Imp gal (85 l) of nitrous oxide (GM 1) and 15.4 Imp gal (70 l) of methanol-water (MW 50), which injected into the Jumo 213E engine according to the altitude at which the fighter was flying, boosted output mightily. Perhaps this was the clue as to why the Ta 152H-1 was never really put through its paces in the UK – we had no GM 1 or MW 50 at Farnborough! Nevertheless, lack of nitrous oxide and methanol-water notwithstanding, my adrenalin began to flow that summer morning as I eased myself into the cockpit of Ta 152H-1 Werk-Nr 150168 and peered along that immense nose which stretched out so far ahead of the windscreen – the only aircraft I was ever to fly offering a comparable stretch of nose was the Blackburn Firebrand. The German fighter was, of course, equipped with a pressurised cabin and since I had done quite a bit of flying in the pressurised Spitfire XIX on clean air and turbulence investigation, the opportunity given by the flight to Brize Norton to make a comparison between the German and British fighters was irresistible.

The take-off of the Ta 152H-1 was shorter than that of the Spitfire XIX and the climb was steeper albeit somewhat slower than that of the British fighter, but once the 30,000 ft (9 145 m) mark had slipped past the altimeter, the Tank fighter gave me the impression of holding its rate of climb better than its British counterpart. In so far as maneuverability was concerned, the story was very much the same; the Spitfire was certainly the better of the two below 30,000 ft (9 145 m), there being little to choose between British and German fighters between that altitude and 35,000 ft (10 760m), but above the latter altitude the Ta 152H-1 enjoyed a decided edge. I gave the German fighter its head on the way to Brize Norton and did a full throttle run at 35,000 ft (10 670 m), which, by my rough reckoning, worked out at around 425 mph (684 km/h), or about 35 mph (56 km/h) less than the Spitfire XIX was capable of, but, of course, the availability of GM 1 boost would have more than redressed the balance and the Ta 152H-1 was certainly the superior aeroplane on the score of range. In essence, however, these two potential opponents were remarkably close from many aspects, illustrating how closely parallel Britain and Germany were running in piston-engined fighter technology.

On the descent from altitude to Brize Norton, I had time to make quick checks on the stability and control of the German fighter. I found a noticeable reduction in roll rate and an increase in the stick force per g by comparison with its BMW 801-powered predecessors, some of the more attractive qualities of the original fighter having been sacrificed in order to achieve the best possible performance at extreme altitudes. I therefore expected the stability to be improved over that of the Fw 190, as indeed it was, but it was not so good that a protracted flight at 45,000 ft (13 715 m) would not have been a fatiguing experience, a fact evidently recognised by the provision of an autopilot.

The landing at Brize Norton from an approach at 118 mph (190 km/h) was straightforward enough although I took the precaution of landing off a curved final to see round that fantastic nose. With its wide-track undercarriage,

Ofw. Walter Loos from Stab JG 301 shot down four Allied aircraft while flying the Ta 152 H. On April 20, 1945 he was decorated with the Knights Cross. Loss was credited with 38 kills, including 22 USAAF heavy bombers.

Ofw. Willi Reschke, Knights Cross, from JG 301 shot down four enemy aircraft at the controls of the Ta 152 H. During the war Reschke scored 27 aerial victories, including 20 heavy bomber kills. He himself was shot down no fewer than eight times and had to bail out on four occasions.

Technical specifications of the Focke-Wulf Ta 152 H

An oil painting showing Ofw. Willi Reschke's victory over a Yak-9 on April 24, 1945. The piece by Manfred Schröder is currently part of Peter Neuwerth's collection.

This Focke-Wulf Ta 152 H-1, W.Nr. 150 167 was captured by U.S. forces at Erfurt-Nord.

the aircraft felt very stable on the landing run, a characteristic for which I was to be thankful some weeks later, after the powers-that-be had decided that our Ta 152H-1 should take its place in the static park of the Exhibition of German Aircraft and Equipment that was being organised at Farnborough.

On 22 October 1945, I returned to Brize Norton to bring the Ta 152H-1 back to Farnborough for the exhibition, the fighter having been in storage since I had delivered it there on 18 August. Needless to say, I gave the aircraft a pretty thorough pre-flight check and engine run-up before taking-off for Farnborough. In the event, the flight was uneventful, but once I touched down on Farnborough's main runway and began to apply the foot brakes I immediately realised that these were very weak indeed. In fact, they faded away rapidly to zero effectiveness. A slight swing started to develop and I let this go enough to steer me on to the grass in order to slow the aircraft. I then applied full opposite rudder to prevent a ground loop developing. After a few adrenalin-pumping seconds, the Ta 152H-1 slowed gently to a standstill.

In my view, the Ta 152H-1 was every bit as good as any of its Allied piston-engined counterparts and, from some aspects, better than most. It was unfortunate for the Jagdflieger but undoubtedly fortunate for the Allies that it arrived on the scene too late to play any serious role in the air war."[12]

At some point the British were also in possession of another Ta 152 example, the Ta 152 H-0, W.Nr. 150 006, "green 6", which was captured at Leck. Between January 22 and 23, 1946 the aircraft was transported by road to Schleswig, but ultimately it never arrived in the UK. It was most likely scrapped later somewhere in Germany.

Technical specifications of the Focke-Wulf Ta 152 H

The Focke-Wulf Ta 152 H high-altitude fighter was a single seat monoplane featuring retractable landing gear and pressurized cockpit.

The semi-monocoque fuselage was manufactured from steel and aluminum and featured structural members including frames and longerons. There were fourteen fuselage frames, including frame 1 where the engine firewall was installed and frame 14 where the tail section was attached. The fuselage consisted of four separate sections attached by bolts and rivets.

Compared to a stock Focke-Wulf Fw 190 A, the Ta 152's forward fuselage section was extended by 0.672 m to allow the installation of the MK 108 30 mm cannon. To simplify the manufacturing process the forward fuselage section was bolted to the engine mount attach-

Technical specifications of the Focke-Wulf Ta 152 H

Another photograph of the same machine. Notice the characteristic wide wooden blades of the VS 9 propeller.

ment points. The mid section of the forward fuselage housed the forward wing spar, which was moved forward by 0.420 m to compensate for the altered CG location. With the wings moved forward the rear spar was also relocated and attached to fuselage frame 4. The forward fuselage fuel tank was also moved and its covers and fuselage skin panels in that area had to be redesigned.

In order to preserve the aircraft's directional stability after the extension of the forward fuselage, a 0.50 m fuselage plug was added to the tail section. The plug could now accommodate compressed air and oxygen bottles that had to be moved from the front to maintain proper airframe balance. The longer fuselage required the use of steel longerons in place of previously used duralumin units.

The mid fuselage section housed a pressurized cockpit located just above the aft fuselage fuel tank. The cockpit was built around a steel frame. Instrument panel was attached to

National markings on this Ta 152 H-1, W.Nr. 150 167 were painted using only black paint (RLM 22 Schwarz).

Focke-Wulf Ta 152 — 49

Technical specifications of the Focke-Wulf Ta 152 H

The aircraft in the background, on the left hand side, is the Ta 152 H-1, W.Nr. 150 167 that met its end in a scrap yard.

Two Canadian soldiers strike a pose in front of a Ta 152 H-1 captured at Leck in May 1945.

a bulkhead at frame 3, while the pilot's seat was mounted on frame 5. The windshield assembly was attached to the top of fuselage frame 3. The canopy transparencies were supported by a welded steel frame that also functioned as a roll bar. The front windshield pane was electrically heated to prevent icing and fogging. The side canopy panels were made of laminated glass. The pilot's seat consisted of a duralumin tub attached in four points to a pair of steel beams. The left side of the fuselage featured a fold-out step allowing easier access to the cockpit. DKH-Paste 8800 sealant was used in the installation of canopy transparencies. The canopy was sealed via a circular tube filled with foam rubber which was inflated by a compressed air bottle to 2.5 atm. The one-liter bottle allowed 80 pressurization cycles. In emergency the cockpit was first depressurized, than the canopy locks were released before the unit was finally jettisoned. The windscreen was of a double-pane design with a 6 mm (.32 in) thick outer pane and a 3 mm inner pane with a 6 mm gap. The gap was fitted with eight silica-gel capsules to absorb any moisture forming between the panes.

Radio compartment cover on the left side of rear fuselage section was sealed with a rubber ring as were the access panels of fuselage mounted MG 151/20 cannons.

The wing was technologically very similar to that used on Focke-Wulf Fw 190 A fighters and was of entirely metal design. To allow a better access to the engine bay area the main landing gear attachment points were moved outboard by 0.250 m. This arrangement was made possible by extending the wing spar by 0.5 m. The fuselage-wing area had to be also redesigned. The aircraft's wing had a span of 14.82 m and area of 23.5 m. The new wing required strengthened skin panels near the fuselage. Additional reinforcement was required in the area of the wing holding unprotected bag fuel tanks. The wing surfaces featured many access panels to allow easier servicing by the ground crews.

The landing gear was extended and retracted hydraulically, as opposed to the electrical system used on the Fw 190 A. The main landing gear legs were attached to the forward wing spar. The aircraft featured VDM 8-2092 A-1 main landing gear wheel with 740 x 210 mm tires. Split wheel well duralumin fairings were attached to each main landing gear strut. Additional landing gear doors covered inboard part of the wheel wells. In the case of hydraulic system failure the landing gear could be ex-

Technical specifications of the Focke-Wulf Ta 152 H

tended using emergency compressed air bottle. The tail wheel manufactured by KPZ had a 380 x 150 mm tire and retracted partially into the tail section. Upon extension of the main landing gear the tail wheel locks were released and the wheel extended under its own weight.

The horizontal stabilizer assembly was adopted directly from the Fw 190 A, while the vertical fin was enlarged to provide better stability. To simplify the assembly process vertical stabilizer and the 0.5 m fuselage extension plug were manufactured as a single unit. Horizontal stabilizer featured adjustable rigging angle which could be set using a wheel mounted in the cockpit.

Flight control surfaces were enlarged to correspond to the new, longer wing. Trailing edge flaps were also modified with hydraulically powered actuation mechanism. The arrangement of flight control system was otherwise identical to the Fw 190 A.

The Ta 152 H was powered by a propulsion system known as Jäger-Einheitstriebwerk 9-8213 FH 1. It consisted of the Jumo 213 E-1 engine, radiator assembly and engine cowling. Jumo 213 E-1 was a 12-cylinder inverted V engine with internal annular coolant radiator consisting of as many as four sections. Each cylinder was connected to an independent exhaust manifold. The two stage, three speed supercharger provided maximum power output at 10 000m. The engine delivered 1 730 HP at 3 250 rpm at sea level and 1 260 HP at 10 000 m.

In order to provide additional boost at altitudes below 10 000 m the aircraft was equipped with MW 50 methanol-water injection system. The mixture was usually carried in one of the soft fuel bladders in the port wing. A supply of 70 l of the water-methanol mixture was sufficient for 28 minutes of continuous operation of the system. Direct injection of the water-methanol mixture increased engine boost pressure and also improved powerplant cooling.

The aircraft was also equipped with the nitrous oxide power boost system designed to improve engine performance at altitudes above 10 000 m. The GM-1, often dubbed *Göring-Mischung* (Göring's mixture) by Luftwaffe personnel, had a supply of 85 l of nitrous oxide which

This Focke-Wulf Ta 152 H-1, W.Nr. 150 169, sans the propeller, was photographed at Leck after the end of hostilities.

The Focke-Wulf Ta 152 H-1, W.Nr. 150 168, former "green 9" from Stab JG 301 was displayed among other ex-Luftwaffe machines at Farnborough in 1946.

Technical specifications of the Focke-Wulf Ta 152 H

The Ta 152 H-0, W.Nr. 150 010, CW+CJ from Stab JG 301 is still wearing the RAF markings prior to handover to the Americans on September 4, 1945.

Another shot of the same aircraft.

translated into 17 minutes of continuous use. The mixture was carried in a cylindrical tank located in the mid fuselage section, just aft of the cockpit. The GM-1 could boost the engine's power output by as much as 410 HP.

Engine lubrication system used oil stored in a 72 l tank mounted in the forward fuselage section, just right of the MK 108 cannon. The front of the steel tank was protected by the engine block. Typically, the oil tank was filled with 61 l of engine oil.

In order to obtain optimum firing characteristics of the engine-mounted MK 108 cannon the engine block was tilted downwards by 1° in relation to the longitudinal axis. The all-up weight of the powerplant was 1 520 kg, while the dry weight was 1 403 kg.

The engine drove a three-bladed constant speed propeller with hydraulic governor system. The wooden Junkers VS 9 prop had a diameter of 3.6 m. In later production examples the VS 9 propeller was to be replaced by the smaller diameter (3.5 m) VS 19 unit. To accommodate the installation of the MK 108 cannon the propeller hub featured a gun port connected to a hollow duct to protect against the shockwave associated with the firing of the gun.

Jumo 213 E-1 used B4 aviation fuel carried in two main tanks: forward 232 l fuselage tank (adopted directly from the Fw 190 A) and aft tank holding 360 l of fuel. The aft fuselage tank was located immediately behind the forward unit and extended back to fuselage bulkhead 8. In H-1 models the aft tank was never filled to full capacity in order to maintain proper CG limits. It was typically filled with 260 liters of fuel. The fuel tanks were manufactured of steel sheets (12 mm thick at the top and 16 mm thick on the sides and bottom). An 85 l cylindrical tank holding nitrous oxide for the GM-1 installation was located in the fuselage, just aft of the cockpit, attached to bulkhead 8. The tank could also be used to store additional fuel.

The Ta 152 H-0, W.Nr. 150 010 tied down at a ramp.

Both H-0 and H-1 variants could carry additional 300 l of fuel in a drop tank attached to a Schloß 503 rack mounted on the centerline station. The Ta 152 H-1s could be equipped with six unprotected bag fuel tanks installed inside the wing. The wing tanks had a capacity of 75 l each. Typically one of the wing tanks was used to store 75 liters of methanol-water mixture used in the MW 50 system. The fuel in the wing tanks could be jettisoned by operating a control lever on the left side of the cockpit which activated fuel dump valves. Fuel to the engine was typically provided from the forward fuselage tank. Once the fuel quantity in the forward tank dropped to 160 l, the fuel was cross-fed from the aft tank. The drop tank fuel was used once the aft tank fuel quantity had dropped below 260 l. The maximum fuel capacity was 1 277 l or 1 017 l of fuel plus 85l of nitrous oxide and 75 l of water-methanol mixture.

The Ta 152 H carried one engine-mounted MK 108 30 mm cannon with a design rate of fire of 600 rounds per minute. The gun was pneumatically charged and featured electric ignition. The supply of ammunition was limited to 90 rounds. The cannon was charged using a button on the instrument panel. The B-1 button on the control column activated the trigger mechanism.

A pair of synchronized MG 151/20 20 mm cannons was installed in the wing roots. The weapons were fitted in ports cut in the main wing spar. The guns were charged and fired electrically and were fed from magazines containing 175 rounds per gun. The guns were operated by pressing button A on the control column's grip. The wing guns were synchronized with a BSK 16 gun camera installed in the left wing root. The camera used 15 m of 16 mm film, which allowed three and a half minutes of continuous operation.

Cockpit pressurization was achieved via engine-driven Knorr-Roots-Atemluftverdichter 300/10 compressor. The compressor was designed to kick in above 8 000 meters and provided constant cabin pressure of 0.36 atm. The compressor intake was located in front of the radiator. The air was fed into the cockpit through a filter, a return valve and a regulator assembly. The compressor did not operate below 8 000 m and in such cases the air entered the cockpit directly through an air duct, which would automatically close each time the compressor kicked in.

The Ta 152 H was equipped with FuG 16 ZY radio and an FuG 25a IFF set. Additional avionics mounted in the H-0/R11 and H-1/R11 variants included FuG 125 sets (30 – 33.3 MHz and 200 km operating range) and LGW K 23 autopilot.

Both cockpit and engine compartment featured armored protection. The cockpit armor weighed in at 61 kg (shoulder armor – 4 and 5

Focke-Wulf Ta 152 H-0 and H-1: performance and technical specifications		
	Ta 152 H-0	Ta 152 H-1
Wingspan	14.44 m	14.44 m
Wing area	23.30 m^2	23.30 m^2
Length	10.71 m	10.71 m
Height	3.36 m	3.36 m
Horizontal stabilizer span	3.65 m	3.65 m
Normal operating gross weight	4 727	5 217
Powerplant	Junkers Jumo 213 E-1	Junkers Jumo 213 E-1
Maximum take-off weight	1 750 HP	1 750 HP
Maximum speed (military power) at 10 700 m	706 km/h	697 km/h
Maximum speed (WEP) at 10 700 m	718 km/h	709 km/h
Maximum speed with MW 50 injection at 9 500 m	–	732 km/h
Maximum speed with GM-1 boost at 12 500 m	–	755 km/h
Operating ceiling	13 650 m	14 200 m
Maximum range	850 km	1215 km

Paint and camouflage schemes

The Ta 152 H-0, W.Nr. 150 010 photographed at Wright Field. Notice the FE-112 stenciled on the vertical fin.

This picture of the Ta 152 H-0, W.Nr. 150 010 shows the characteristic saw tooth camouflage pattern on the wing's leading edge.

mm plates weighing 5.8 kg; seat armor – 8 mm plates, 19.1 kg; additional armor – 5 mm plate, 8.6 kg; head protection – 12 mm armor, 13 kg; windshield – 50 mm armored glass, 14.5 kg). The armor around the engine and oil tank weighed 59 kg (5 and 12 mm armor plate around the engine – 50 kg and 8 mm armor around the oil tank weighing 9 kg). Total armor weight was 120 kg.

Paint and camouflage schemes

Most Focke-Wulf Fw 190 airframes involved in the high-altitude fighter program between 1942 and 1944 wore standard Luftwaffe camouflage used in that period. In May 1942 the RLM published official guidelines for application of camouflage schemes on various aircraft types (HM-Anweisung Nr. 7/42), which specified that all Fw 190 fighters should be painted in keeping with an instruction first introduced in November 1941 (Dienstvorschrift L.Dv. 521/1). The guidelines called for a camouflage scheme consisting of two shades of grey (RLM 74 Graugrün and RLM 75 Grauviolett) on upper surfaces of wings, horizontal stabilizer and the fuselage. Fuselage sides, as well as lower wing and horizontal stabilizer surfaces were to be sprayed with gray-blue paint (RLM 76 Lichtblau[13]). Additionally, small patches of RLM 70 Schwarzgrün, RLM 02 Grau and RLM 75 Grauviolett were to be applied to fuselage side surfaces. The mottle on the fuselage sides was also applied using other paints, most typically RLM 74 replacing RLM 70.

The camouflage arrangements used on the upper surfaces of Focke-Wulf Fw 190 A, D and Ta 152 C fighters were very similar and did not differ much from the paint schemes first used on the early production Fw 190 A-1 examples, which saw action as early as 1941. This was not so in the case of the Ta 152 H, whose long wings required some modifications of the standard camouflage pattern.

In many cases experimental aircraft wore overall RLM 02 Grau finish. A good example of that paint scheme is the Focke-Wulf Fw 190 V 18/U1, W.Nr. 0040, CF+OY. Interestingly, skin panels in some areas (engine cowling, air intake and cockpit) retained their natural metal finish.

Factory codes (*Stammkennzeichen*) included four-letter combinations applied to fuselage

54

Paint and camouflage schemes

sides and lower wing surfaces in RLM Schwartz. National markings, including *Balkenkreuz* and swastika (*Hakenkreuz*) were painted using black (RLM 22 Schwarz) and white (RLM 21 Weiß) paints. In the second half of the war a simplified cross design was introduced, which consisted of white or black flanks without the black fill. Virtually all production Ta 152 H aircraft featured that simplified design. The swastika was normally painted in solid black.

In mid 1944 the standard Luftwaffe fighter camouflage schemes underwent some major changes. Among the colors introduced in that period and recommended by the RLM in standard camouflage applications were RLM 81 Braunviolett, RLM 82 Hellgrün and RLM 83 Dunkelgrün. RLM 81 was a shade of brown with a hint of violet and resembled pre-war RLM 61 Dunkelbraun. RLM 82 corresponded to the pre-war RLM 62 Grün, while RLM 83 looked similar to RLM 64 Dunkelgrün, also used before the war. RLM 81 and RLM 82 were officially approved for use by the Luftwaffe in an official RLM document (*Sammelmitteilung*) published on July 1, 1944. At the same time the use of RLM 70 Schwarzgrün, RLM 71 Dunkelgrün and RLM 65 Hellblau was discontinued (RLM 70 was retained only for propeller blades). Another document published by the RLM on August 15, 1944 (*Sammelmitteilung 2*) specified that RLM 74 Graugrün be replaced with RLM 83. RLM 75 continued to be used simultaneously with the new colors, which makes it very difficult to establish the actual paints used by the Luftwaffe in the final stages of the war, especially that in most cases only black and white photographs are available. The most commonly used combinations included RLM 81/82, RLM 81/83 or RLM 81/75, but other arrangements, including RLM 82/75, RLM 83/76 and 82/83 were not infrequent.

In March 1944 Focke-Wulf received their first official guidelines on camouflage schemes to be applied to the Ta 152 A fighters (Sichtschutzanstrich Ta 152 (Trag- und Leitwerk) 8-152.960-02). The document specified the exact camouflage pattern to be applied to upper surfaces, which was practically unchanged No. 5 scheme. The colors to be used on upper surfaces were RLM 74 and RLM 75, while side and lower surfaces were to be painted using RLM 76 with spots of RLM 76 added on the sides of the fuselage and vertical fin. The document was modified in November 1944 with the replacement of RLM 74 and RLM 75 with RLM 81 and RLM 82. To simplify the production process the RLM 02 spots on fuselage sides were discarded while lower surfaces were to be left in their original factory finish. Furthermore, RLM 76 paint was to be used exclusively on fuselage side surfaces and on vertical stabilizer. The idea to drop RLM 76 coat from lower surfaces of Fw 190s was first communicated in Focke-Wulf's document sent to Erprobungsstelle Travemünde

Breakdown of aircraft total weight		
Designation	Ta 152 H-0	Ta 152 H-1
Fuselage	412	412
Landing gear	245	245
Tail plane (metal)	136	136
Flight controls	35	35
Wing	629	654
Powerplant (forward of the firewall)	1822	1822
Powerplant ancillary equipment in the fuselage	170	248
Standard equipment	224	247
Auxiliary equipment	233	233
Ballast	14	1
Aircraft empty weight – total	3 920	4 031
Pilot	100	100
Fuel in forward fuselage	172	172
Fuel in aft fuselage	268	268
Fuel in drop tank	85	–
Fuel in four wing tanks (400 l)	–	296
GM-1 mixture in 85 l fuselage tank	–	104
Engine oil	55	55
Ammunition for two MG 151 cannons (175 rounds per barrel)	77	77
Ammunition for MK 108 cannon (90 rounds)	50	50
Total payload	807	1 186
Normal operating gross weight	4 727	5 217

Another photograph of the same aircraft. Today the machine is in storage at NASM in Washington, DC.

Paint and camouflage schemes

A list of Focke-Wulf Ta 152 H production examples manufactured at Cottbus plant

Werknummer	Manufacturer fuselage code	Remarks
150 001	CW+CA	First flight November 24, 1944 at Cottbus. Pilot – Flugkapitän Hans Sander. In service with III./JG 301 from January 27, 1945.
150 002	CW+CB	First flight November 29, 1944 at Cottbus. Pilot – Flugkapitän Hans Sander.
150 003	CW+CC	First flight December 3, 1944 at Cottbus. Pilot – Flugkapitän Hans Sander. Handed over to Erprobungsstelle Rechlin on December 11, 1944. Aircraft received wooden tailplane during later service. From February 4, 1945 in service with Jagdstaffel Ta 152 at Roggenthin, CO: Hptm. Stolle.
150 004	CW+CD	First flight December 17, 1944. Pilot – Flugkapitän Hans Sander. Flight tested at Langenhagen before hand-over to Stab JG 301. Captured by British forces after the war.
150 005	CW+CE	First flown on December 8, 1944 at Cottbus. Transferred to Junkers for engine trials. Last record of the aircraft dated March 18, 1945.
150 006	CW+CF	First recorded flight – transit from Neuhausen to Cottbus on December 27, 1944. Return flight on December 31, 1944. Service trials at Erprobungsstelle Rechlin from February 10 to March 2, 1945. Operational service with Jagdstaffel Ta 152.
150 007	CW+CG, later "black 3"	Delivered to III./JG 301, later Stabsschwarm JG 301, pilot Ofw. Reschke. On March 15, 1945 Gen. Maj. Pelz piloted the aircraft during a test sortie.
150 008	CW+CH	Flight tested at Erprobungsstelle Rechlin. On February 20, 1945 suffered a wheels-up landing accident at Kleinballhausen, pilot Baist. After repairs delivered to Jagdstaffel Ta 152.
150 009	CW+CI	First flight at Cottbus on December 17, 1944. On December 24 delivered to Roggentin, pilot Kamp. Aircraft went on to serve with Jagdstaffel Ta 152.
150 010	CW+CJ	Flight tested at Erprobungsstelle Rechlin from January 30 to March 8, 1945, including trials of wooden tailplane. Aircraft saw operational service with Jagdstaffel Ta 152 and Stab JG 11. Captured by the Allies in Aalborg, Denmark.
150 011	CW+CK	Trials of the GM-1 system at Erprobungsstelle Rechlin, later delivered to Jagdstaffel Ta 152.
150 012		
150 013		First recorded flight on January 2, 1945.
150 014		First flight on December 23, 1944, pilot Bielefeld. On January 5, 1945 the aircraft flew from Cottbus to Neuhausen.
150 015		First recorded flight – ferry to Cottbus from Neuhausen on January 5, 1945.
150 016		First recorded flight – ferry from Neuhausen to Cottbus on December 29, 1944.
150 017		First recorded flight – ferry from Cottbus to Neuhausen on December 29, 1944.
150 018		
150 019		First flight on December 29, 1944, pilot Bielefeld.
150 020	CW+CT	First recorded flight on January 10, 1945.
150 021		First recorded flight on December 31, 1944.
150 022		Collected from Neuhausen on January 10, 1945. Operational service with III./JG 301 from January 27, 1945. Aircraft damaged in a forced landing accident in February 1945, later repaired.
150 023		First flight from Cottbus to Neuhausen on December 29, 1944, pilot Bielefeld. Aircraft was lost on February 9, 1945 when it crashed while flying from Tanewitz to Rechlin, pilot Hptm. Herbert Eggers.
150 024		First flight from Cottbus to Neuhausen on December 31, 1944, pilot Bielefeld.
150 025		First recorded flight on December 31, 1944. Aircraft suffered a 10% damage in a landing accident. After repairs delivered to III./JG 301 on January 27, 1945.
150 026		
150 027		First recorded flight on January 5, 1945 at Neuhausen. Later converted to the Ta 152 C-3 standard powered by the Jumo 213 E. Used in trials of the engine mounted MK 103 30 mm cannon.
150 028		
150 029		First flight at Cottbus on January 7, 1945.
150 030		First recorded flights on February 1 and 2, 1945 at Langenhagen, pilot Hans Sander. Converted to the C-3 variant powered by the Jumo 213 E. Used in trials of the engine mounted MK 103 30 mm cannon.
150 031		
150 032		First flight at Cottbus on January 17, 1945. Delivered to III./JG 301 on January 27, 1945.
150 033		
150 034		First flight from Cottbus to Neuhausen on January 20, 1945. In service with III./JG 301 from January 27, 1945.
150 035		In service with III./JG 301 from January 27, 1945.
150 036		First flight from Cottbus to Neuhausen on January 16, 1945. In service with III./JG 301 from January 27, 1945.
150 037		First flight from Cottbus to Neuhausen on January 18, 1945. In service with III./JG 301 from January 27, 1945.
150 038		In service with III./JG 301 from January 27, 1945.
150 039		In service with III./JG 301 from January 27, 1945.
150 040		In service with III./JG 301 from January 27, 1945.
150 167		Earmarked for conversion to the Ta 152 H-10 standard. Captured by U.S. forces at Erfurt-Nord on April 15, 1945.
150 168	"green 9"	Stabsschwarm JG 301, pilot Ofw. Reschke. Captured at Leck by the British. Flight tested by Eric Brown at Brize Norton, later scrapped in Britain.
150 169		Most likely captured by the British at Leck.

on July 24, 1944 (Fw 190 – Fortfall des Tarnanstriches auf der Flugzeugunterseite). In it Focke-Wulf's management explained that the proposal do discontinue the use of RLM 76 paint on the fighter's lower surfaces was the result of cost and labor-saving analysis performed at the company's Posen plant. Based on that information the RLM instructed the Sorau plant to conduct tests of fifty Fw 190 airframes which were to be delivered with only a coat of primer on the lower surfaces.

However, the early examples of the Ta 152 H-0 (e.g. W.Nr. 150 003, CW+CC, which first flew on December 3, 1944) and the Ta 152 V 7, W.Nr. 110 007, CI+XM (the prototype of the C-0/R11 model first flown on January 8, 1945) featured RLM 75/RLM 83/RLM 76 camouflage, similar to early production examples of the Focke-Wulf Fw 190 D-9.

It appears that first production examples of the Ta 152 H-0 wore camouflage schemes consisting of RLM 75/RLM 83/RLM 76, while the Ta 152 H-1s were most likely painted using RLM 81/82 or RLM 82/83. Most certainly the majority of those aircraft featured RLM 76 paint on their lower surfaces.

Bibliography

Ethell Jeff: *Ta 152, Monogram Closeup 24*, Sturbridge, 1990.
Griehl Manfred, Dressel Joachim: *Focke-Wulf Fw 190/Ta 152, Jäger, Jagdbomber, Panzerjäger*, Stuttgart 1997.
Hermann Dieter: *Focke-Wulf Ta 152: The Story of the Luftwaffe's Late-War High-Altitude Fighter*, Atglen 1999.
Hermann Dietmar: *Focke-Wulf Ta 152: Der Weg zum Höhenjäger*, Oberhaching 1998.
Krzyżan Marian: *Monografie Lotnicze 21 – Fw 190 D, Ta 152*, Gdańsk 1995.
Lowe Malcolm: *Focke-Wulf Ta 152*, Praha 2008.
Murawski Marek J.: *Samoloty Luftwaffe 1933–1945*, Tom 1, Warszawa 1997.
Murawski Marek J., Neuwerth Peter: *JG 301 „Wilde Sau"*, Lublin 2003.
Nohara Shigeru: *Focke-Wulf Fw 190D & Ta 152 Modeling Guide*, Tokyo 2001.
Nowarra Heinz J.: *Focke-Wulf Fw 190, Ta 152, Entwicklung, Technik, Einsatz*, Stuttgart 1987.
Reschke Willy, *Jagdgeschwader 301/302 „Wilde Sau"*, Stuttgart 1998.
Rodeike Peter: *Focke-Wulf Jagdflugzeug Fw 190 A, Fw 190 „Dora", Ta 152 H*, Eutin 1998.

Endnotes

[1] Hermann Dietmar: *Die Focke-Wulf Höhenjäger, Vom ersten Höhenjäger zur Fw 190 H*, Zweibrücken 2002, pp. 97–99.
[2] Hermann Dietmar: *Focke-Wulf Ta 152, Der Weg zum Höhenjäger*, Oberhahing 1998, p. 81.
[3] *Ibidem*, pp. 79–80.
[4] *Ibidem*, p. 81.
[5] Reschke Willi: *Jagdgeschwader 301/302 „Wilde Sau"*, Stuttgart 1998, p. 190.
[6] *Ibidem*.
[7] *Ibidem*, pp. 199–200.
[8] *Ibidem*, pp. 221–222.
[9] *Ibidem*, pp. 229–230.
[10] Rodeike Peter: *Focke-Wulf Jagdflugzeug, Fw 190 A, Fw 190 "Dora", Ta 152 H*, Eutin b.r.w., pp. 416–417.
[11] Reschke..., *op. cit.*, pp. 233–234.
[12] Brown Eric: *Berühmte Flugzeuge der Luftwaffe 1939-1945*, Stuttgart 1988, pp. 132–133.
[13] *RLM 76 Lichtblau came in several shades and was often referred to as Weißblau*, Hellgrau or Hellblau (author's note).

Willi Reschke, chairman of the Fighter Pilots Association of Thuringia (Vorsitzender des Jägerkreises Thüringen) photographed in May 2002 in Ludwigsaus-Friedlos.

Willi Reschke at an annual reunion of former members of JG 301 and JG 302. Potsdam, June 5, 2003.

Focke-Wulf Ta 152

Sheet 1

Ta 152 C-1 – underside

Ta 152 C-1 – top

Drawings: © Stefan Dramiński 2016

KAGERO
1/72 Scale
© Stefan Dramiński 2016

www.kagero.eu
www.shop.kagero.pl

Sheet 2

Focke-Wulf Ta 152

Drawings: © Stefan Dramiński 2016

Ta 152 C-1 – front

Ta 152 C-1 – front

Ta 152 C-1 – rear

Ta 152 C-1 – starboard

Ta 152 C-1 – port

KAGERO 1/72 Scale

© Stefan Dramiński 2016

Sheet 3

Focke-Wulf Ta 152

Monografie Monographs
Drawings: © Stefan Dramiński 2016

Ta 152 H-1 – underside

Ta 152 H-1 – top

KAGERO 1/72 Scale
© Stefan Dramiński 2016

www.kagero.eu
www.shop.kagero.pl

MONOGRAFIE MONOGRAPHS

Focke-Wulf Ta 152

Sheet 4

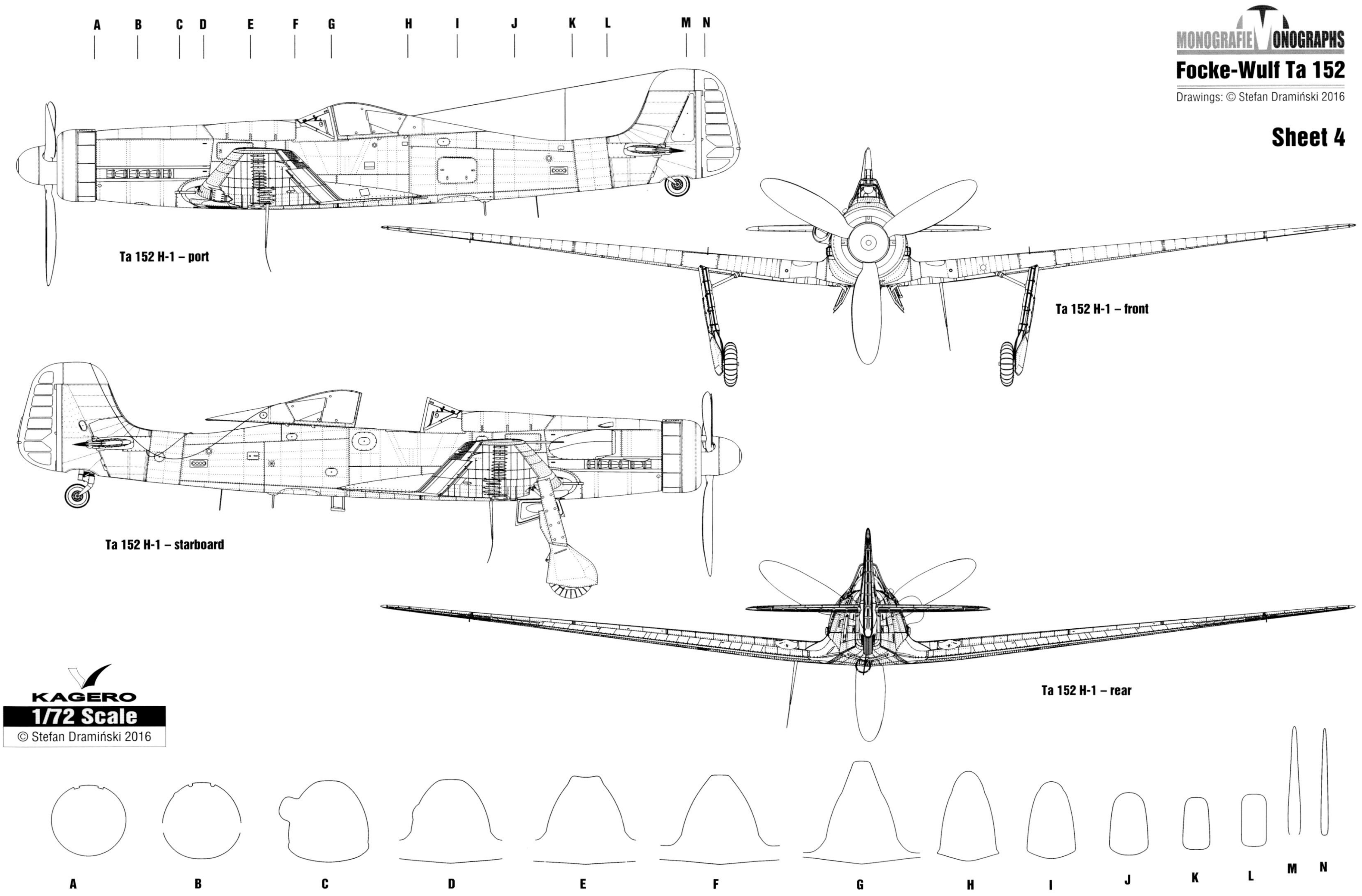

KAGERO
1/72 Scale

Focke-Wulf Ta 152 — Sheet 5

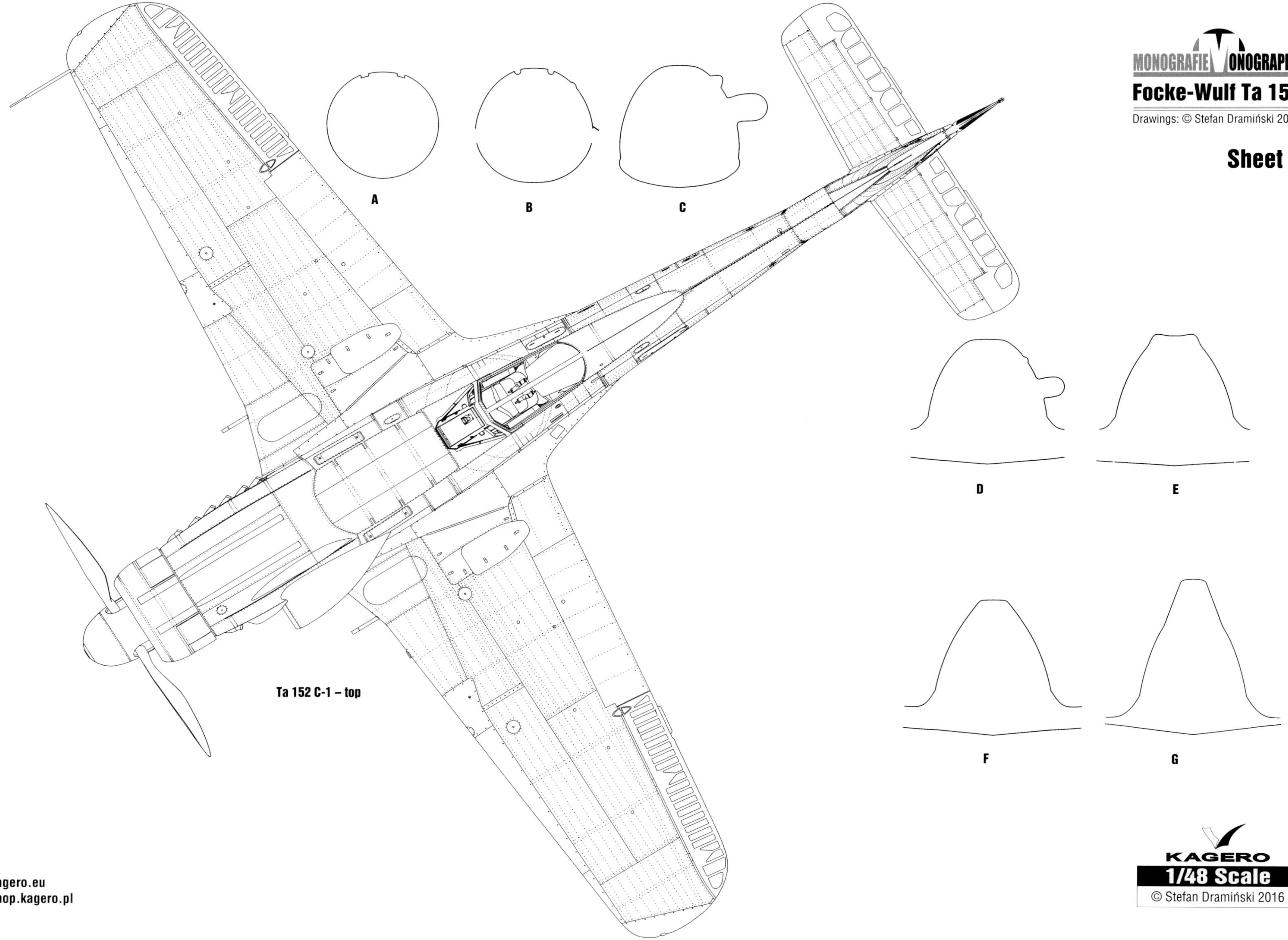

Ta 152 C-1 – top

1/48 Scale

www.kagero.eu
www.shop.kagero.pl

Ta 152 C-1 – underside

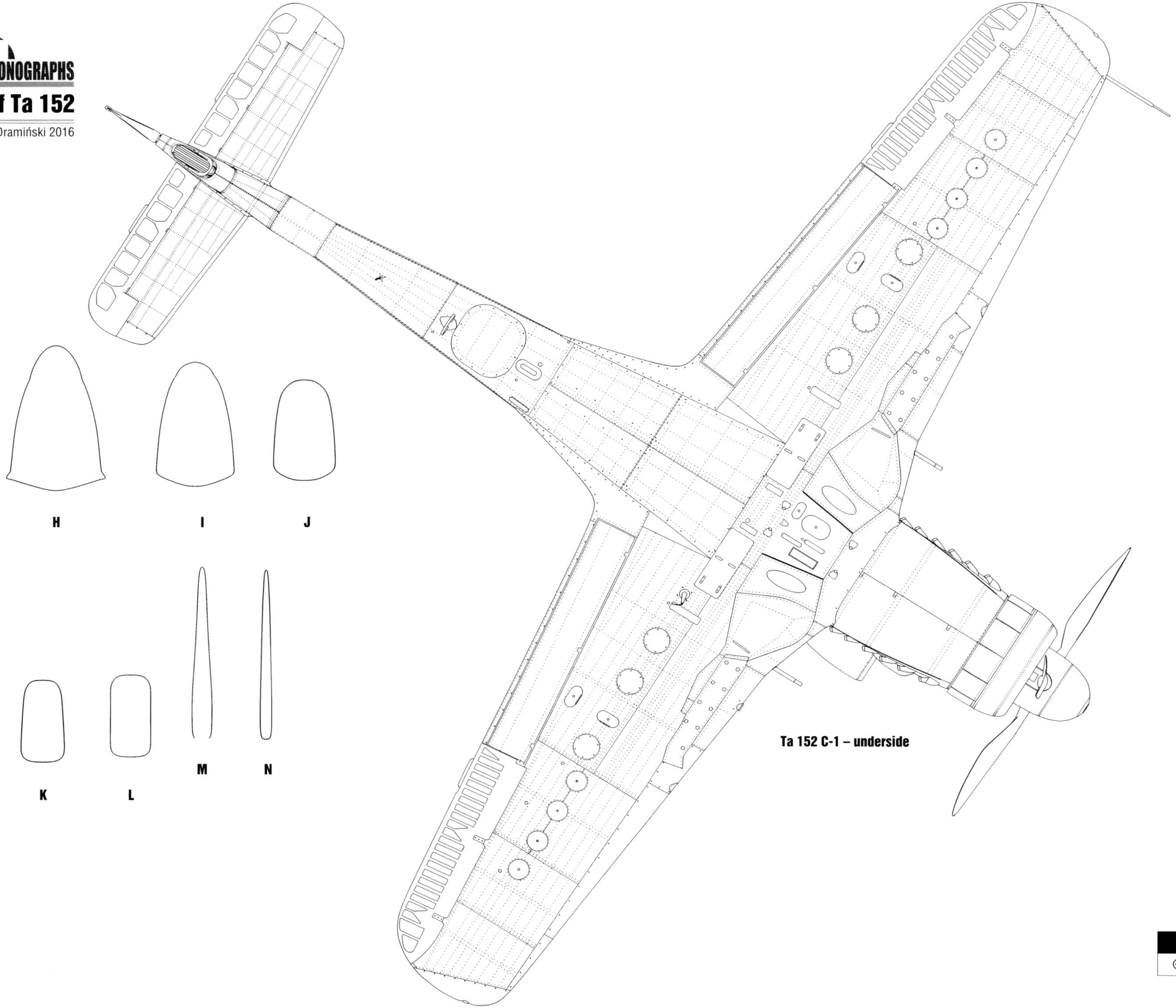

Sheet 7

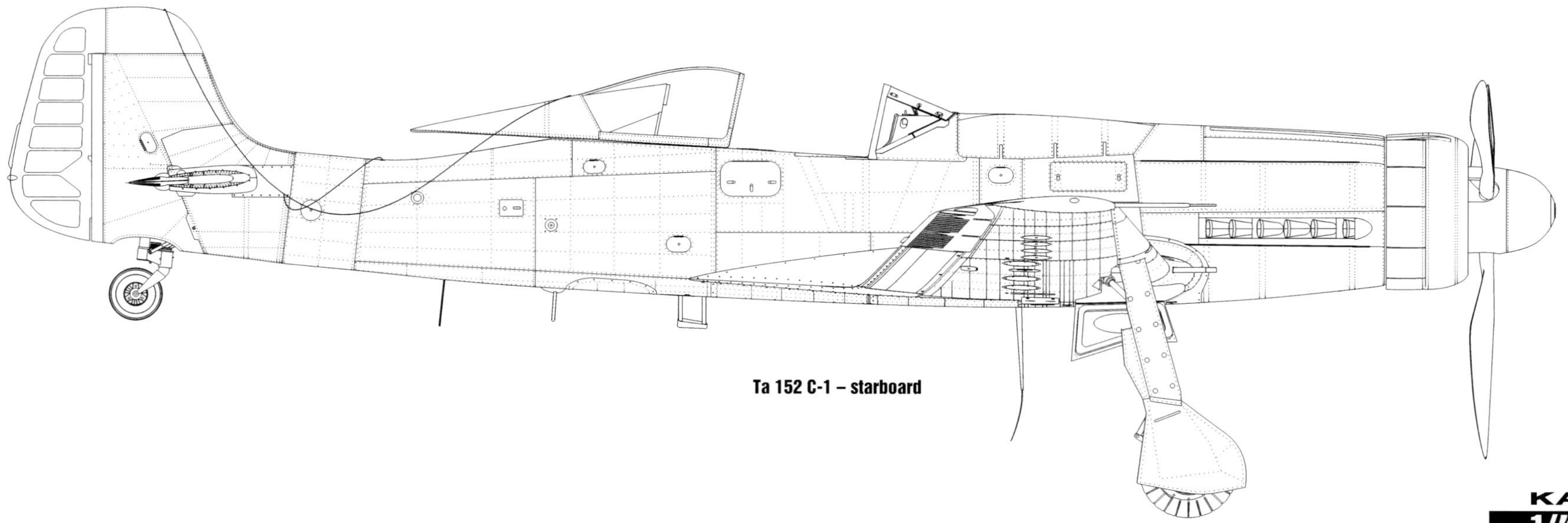

Focke-Wulf Ta 152

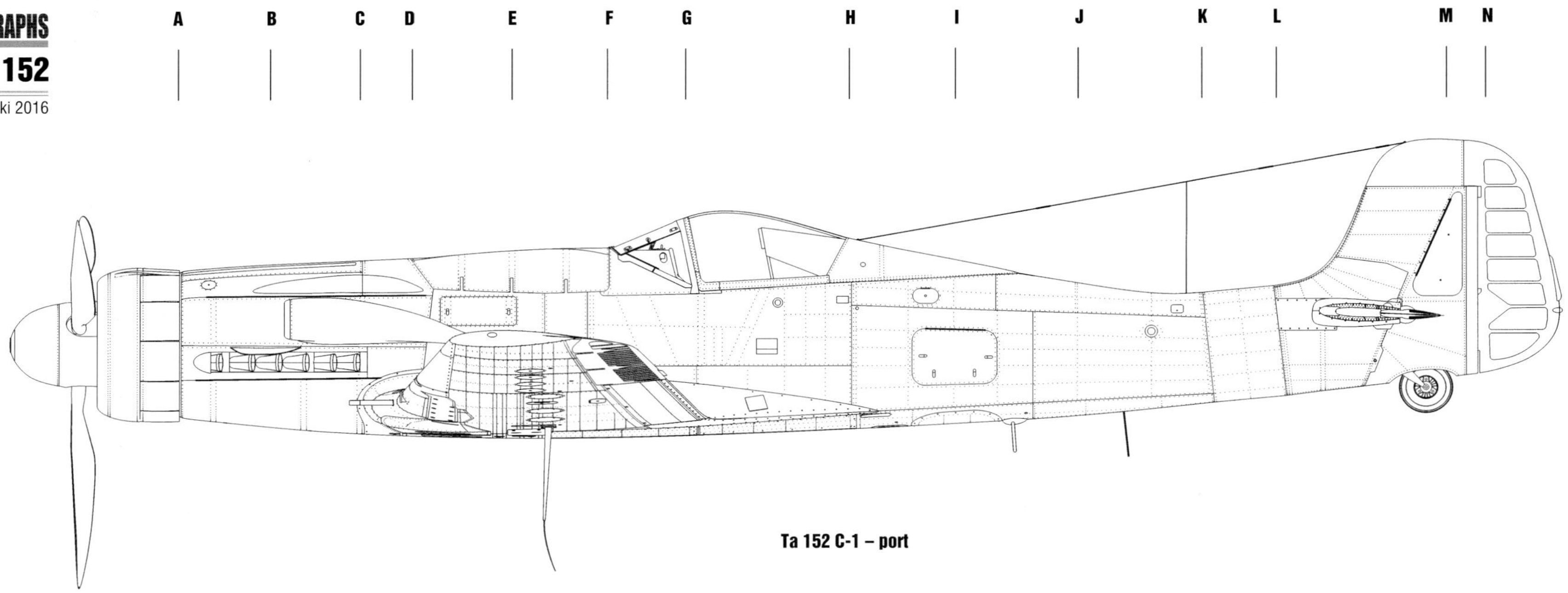

Ta 152 C-1 – port

Ta 152 C-1 – starboard

1/48 Scale

Sheet 8

Focke-Wulf Ta 152

Drawings: © Stefan Dramiński 2016

KAGERO
1/48 Scale
© Stefan Dramiński 2016

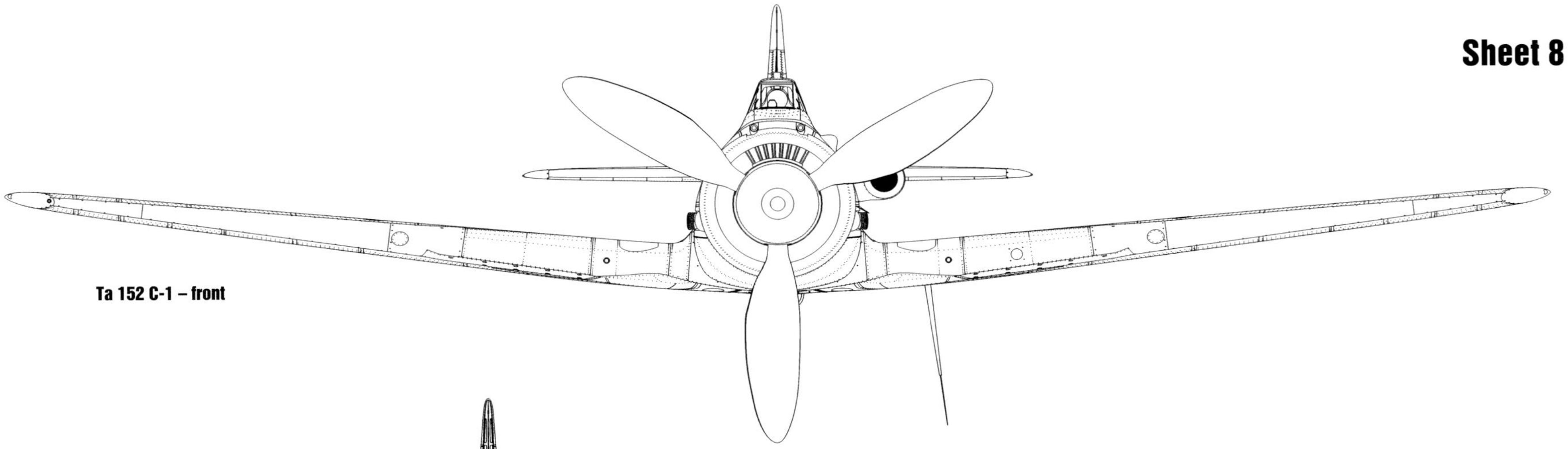

Ta 152 C-1 – front

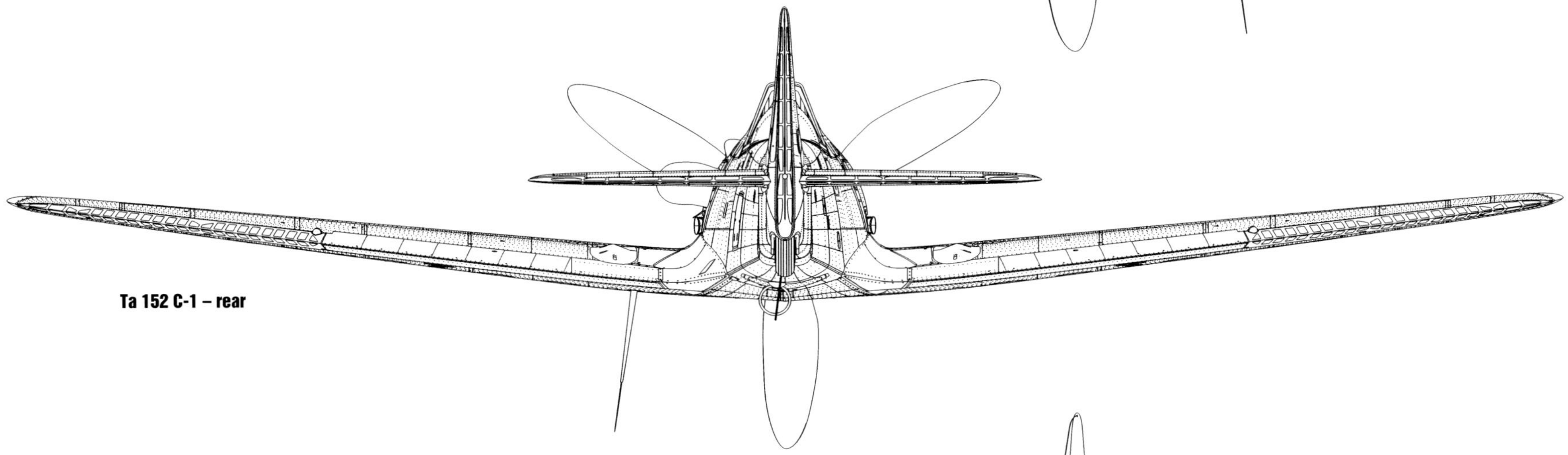

Ta 152 C-1 – rear

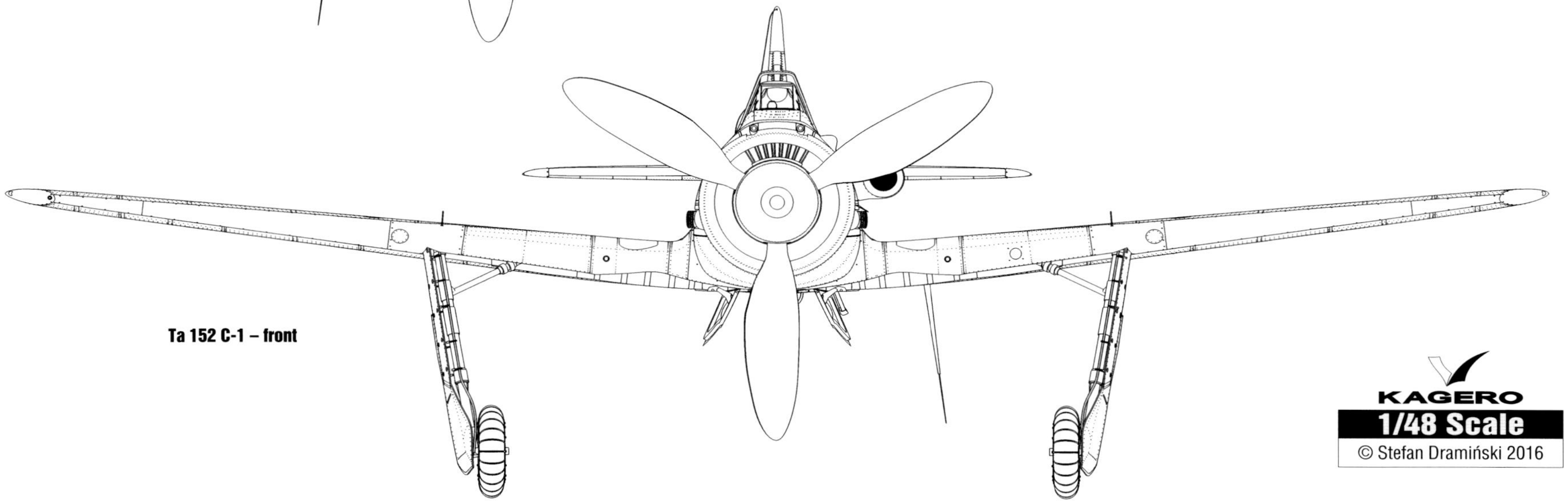

Ta 152 C-1 – front

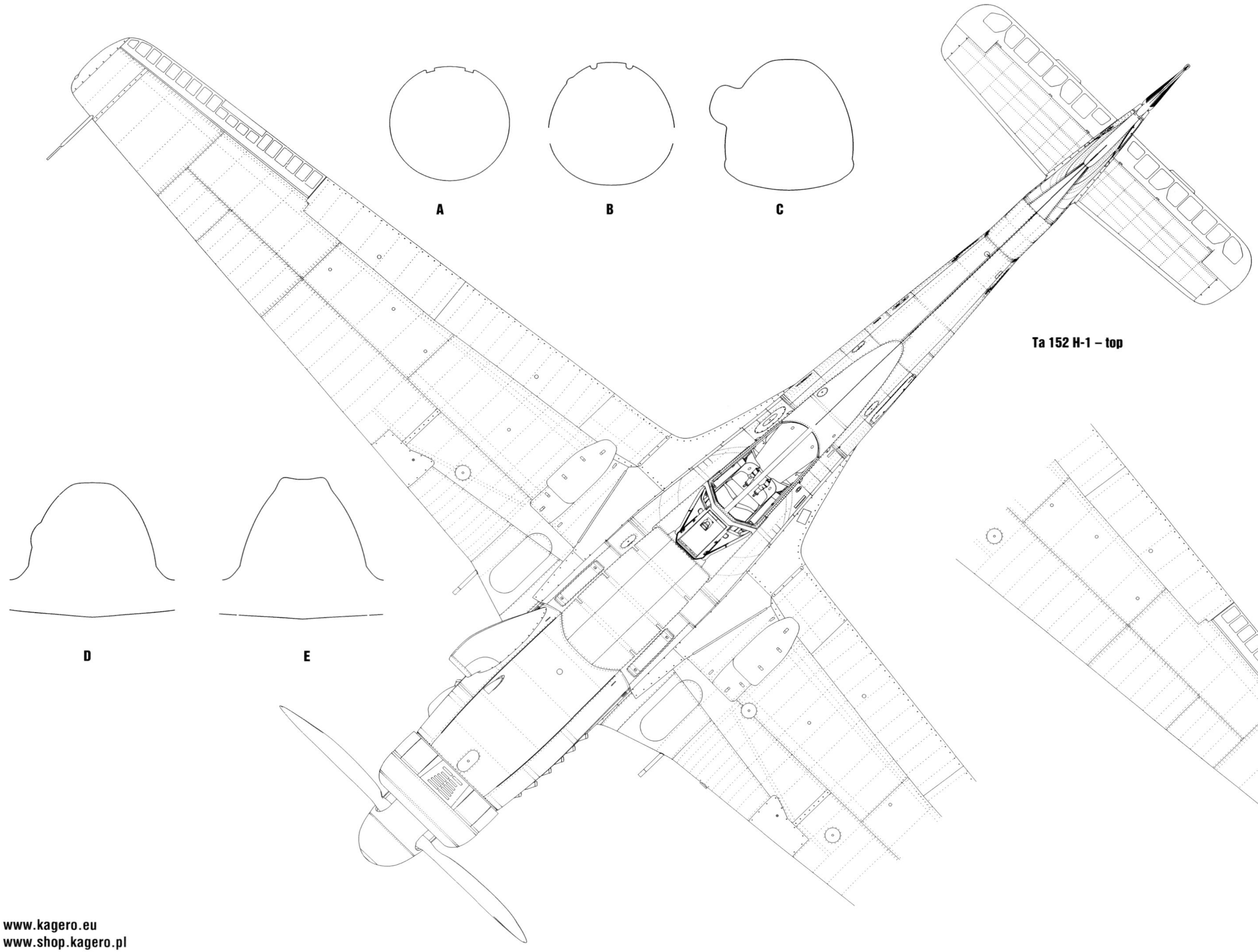

Focke-Wulf Ta 152 — Sheet 9

Ta 152 H-1 – top

1/48 Scale

Sheet 10

Ta 152 H-1 – underside

Focke-Wulf Ta 152
Monografie Monographs
Drawings: © Stefan Dramiński 2016

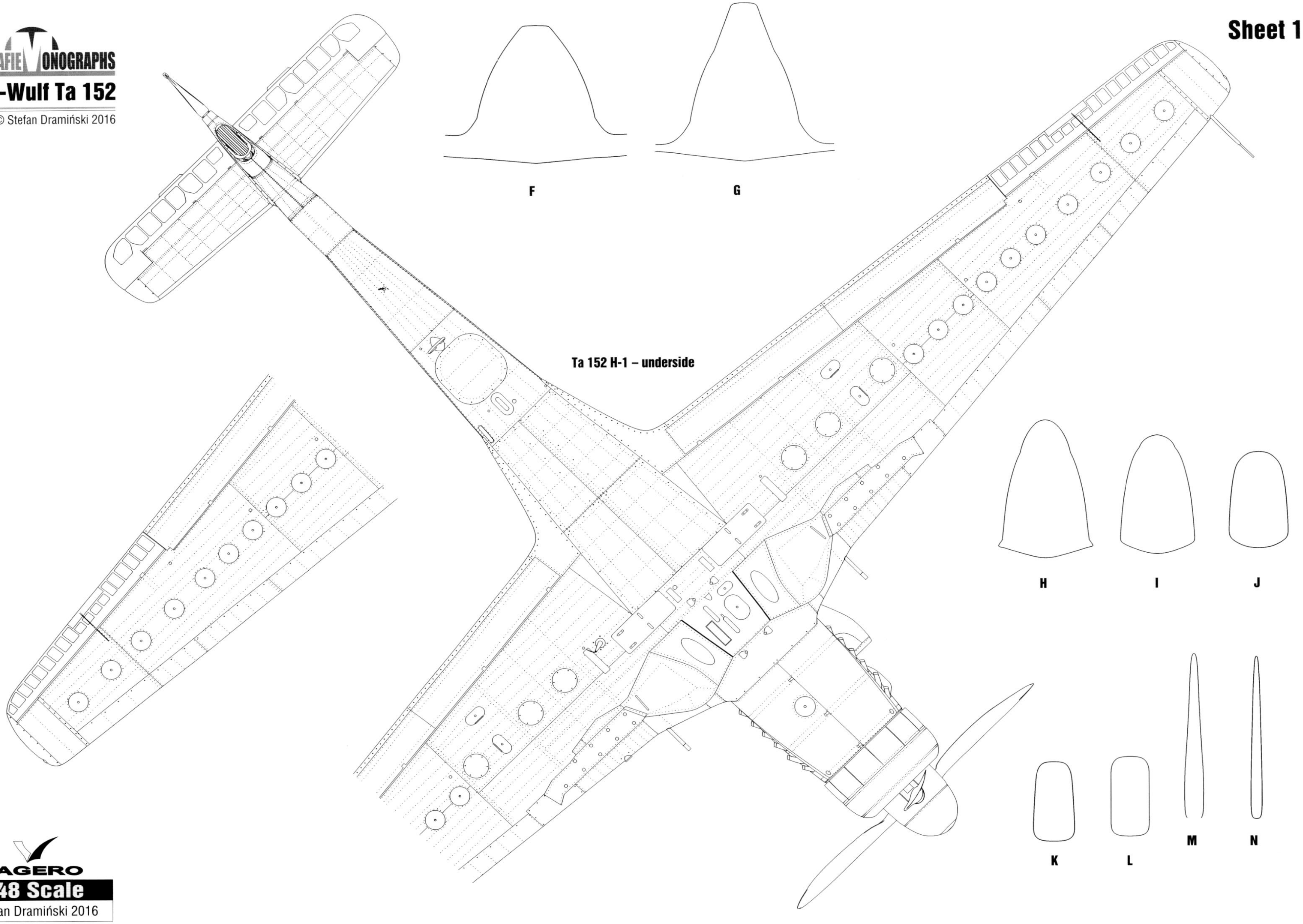

KAGERO
1/48 Scale
© Stefan Dramiński 2016

Focke-Wulf Ta 152

Sheet 11

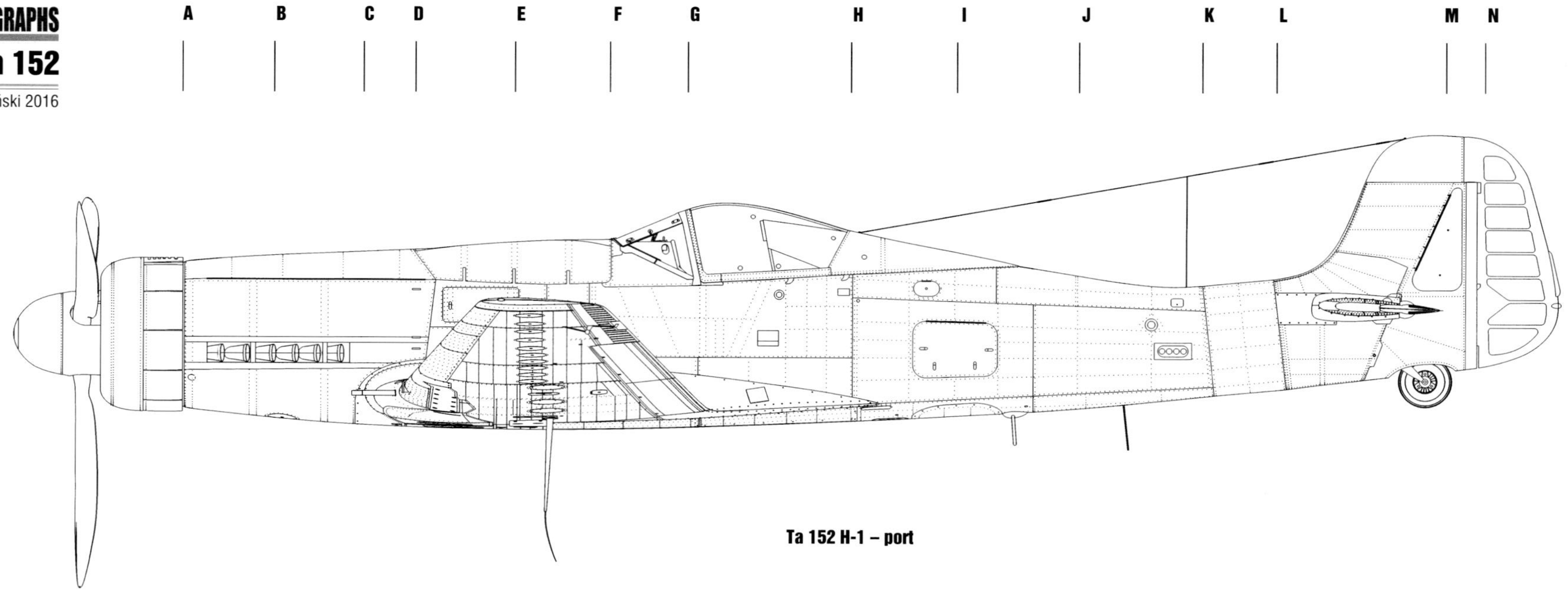

Ta 152 H-1 – port

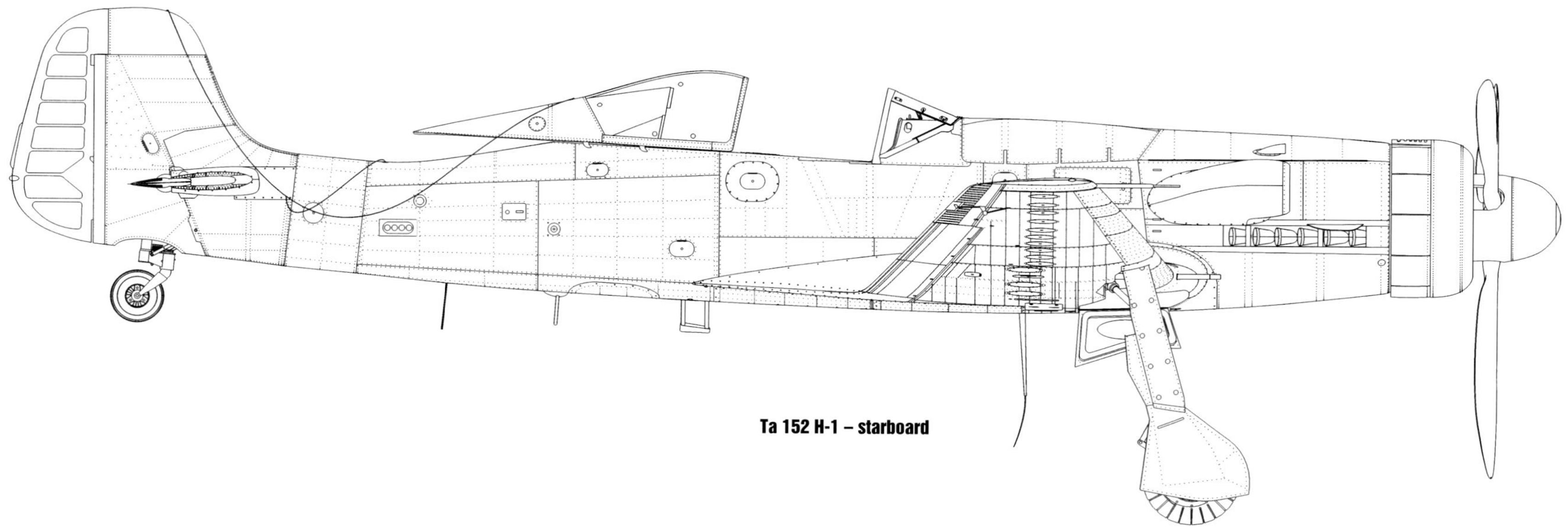

Ta 152 H-1 – starboard

Monografie Monographs
Drawings: © Stefan Dramiński 2016

KAGERO
1/48 Scale
© Stefan Dramiński 2016

www.kagero.eu
www.shop.kagero.pl

Sheet 12

Focke-Wulf Ta 152

monografie Monographs

Drawings: © Stefan Dramiński 2016

Ta 152 H-1 – front

Ta 152 H-1 – front

Ta 152 H-1 – rear

KAGERO
1/48 Scale
© Stefan Dramiński 2016

Focke-Wulf Ta 152 — Sheet 13
Monografie Monographs
Drawings: © Stefan Dramiński 2016

Ta 152 H-1 – top
changes in relation to Ta 152 C-1 are marked in dark color

Ta 152 H-1 – port
changes in relation to Ta 152 C-1 are marked in dark color

Ta 152 H-1 – starboard
changes in relation to Ta 152 C-1 are marked in dark color

KAGERO 1/72 Scale
© Stefan Dramiński 2016

Ta 152 C-1

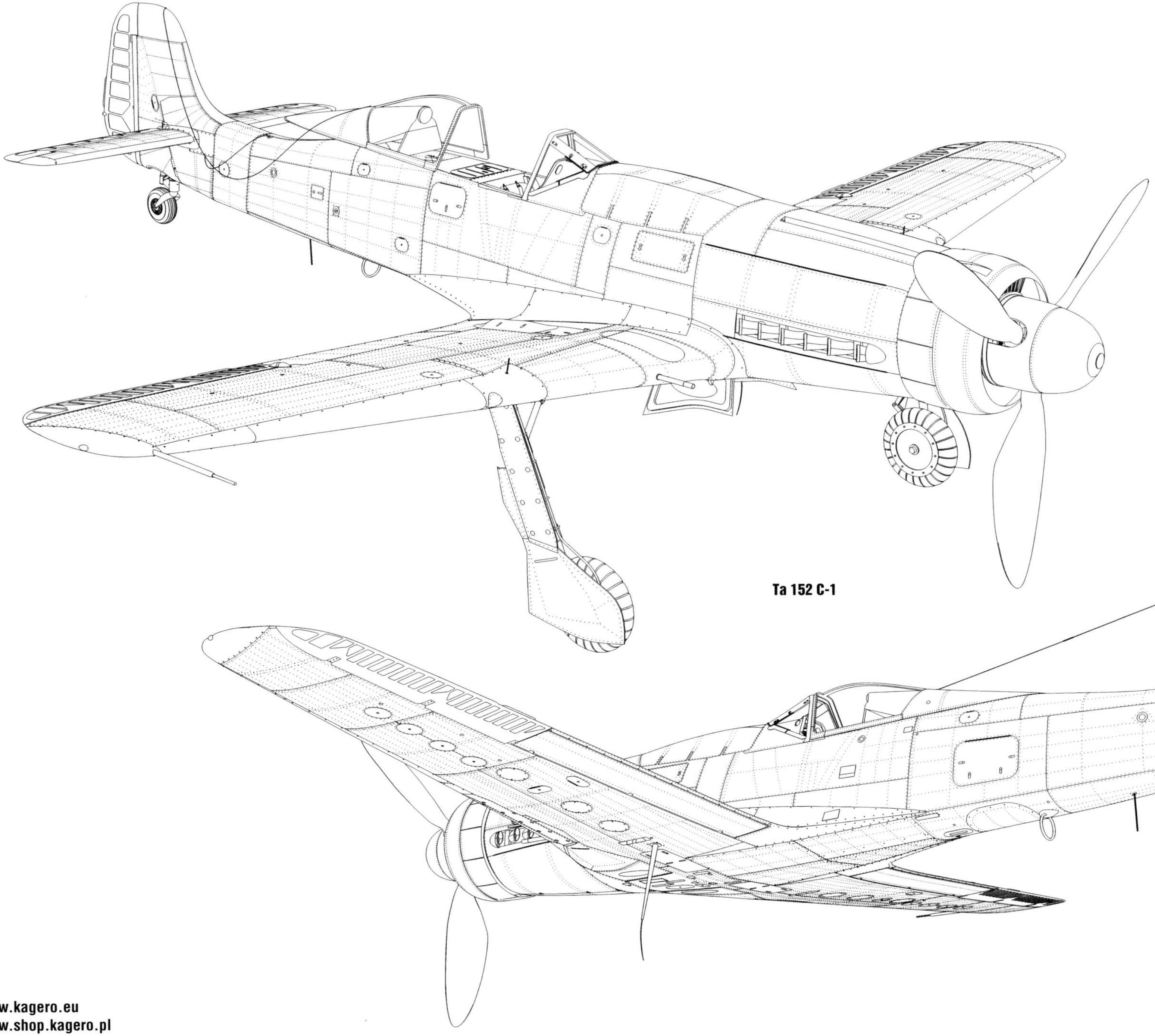

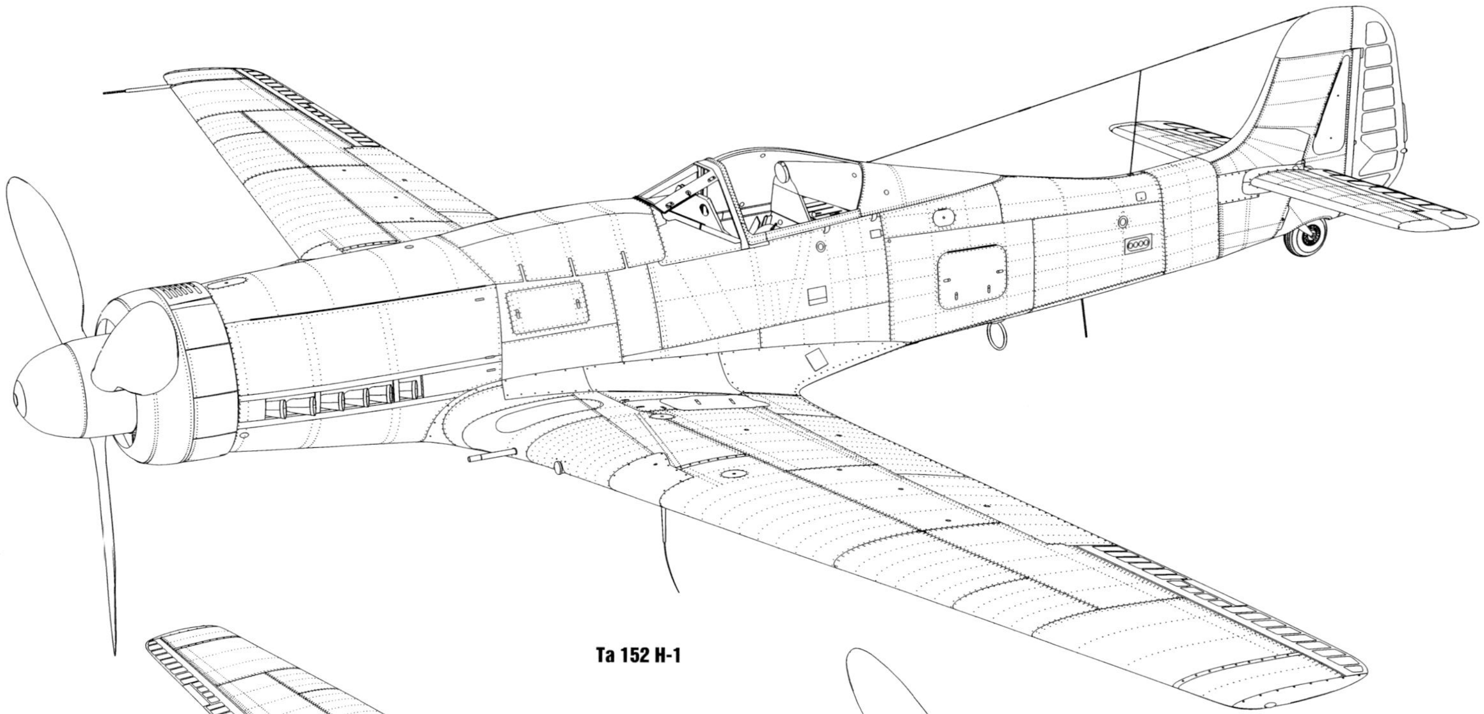

Ta 152 H-1

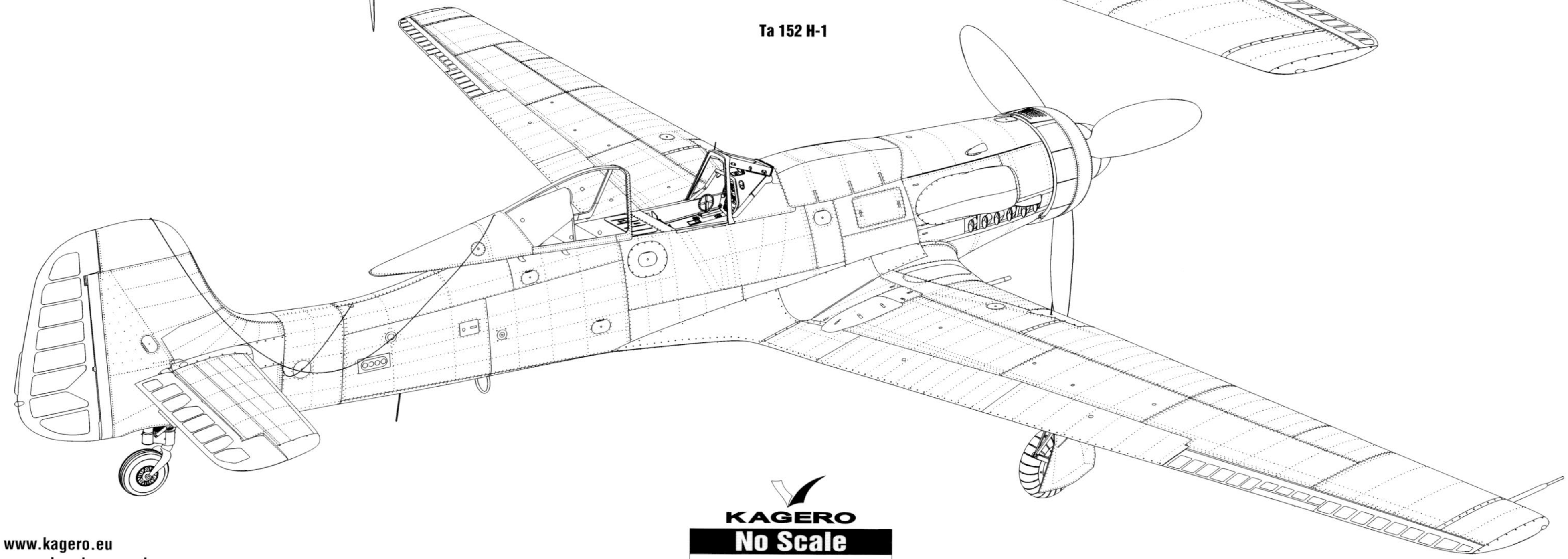

20 mm MG 151/20 cannon

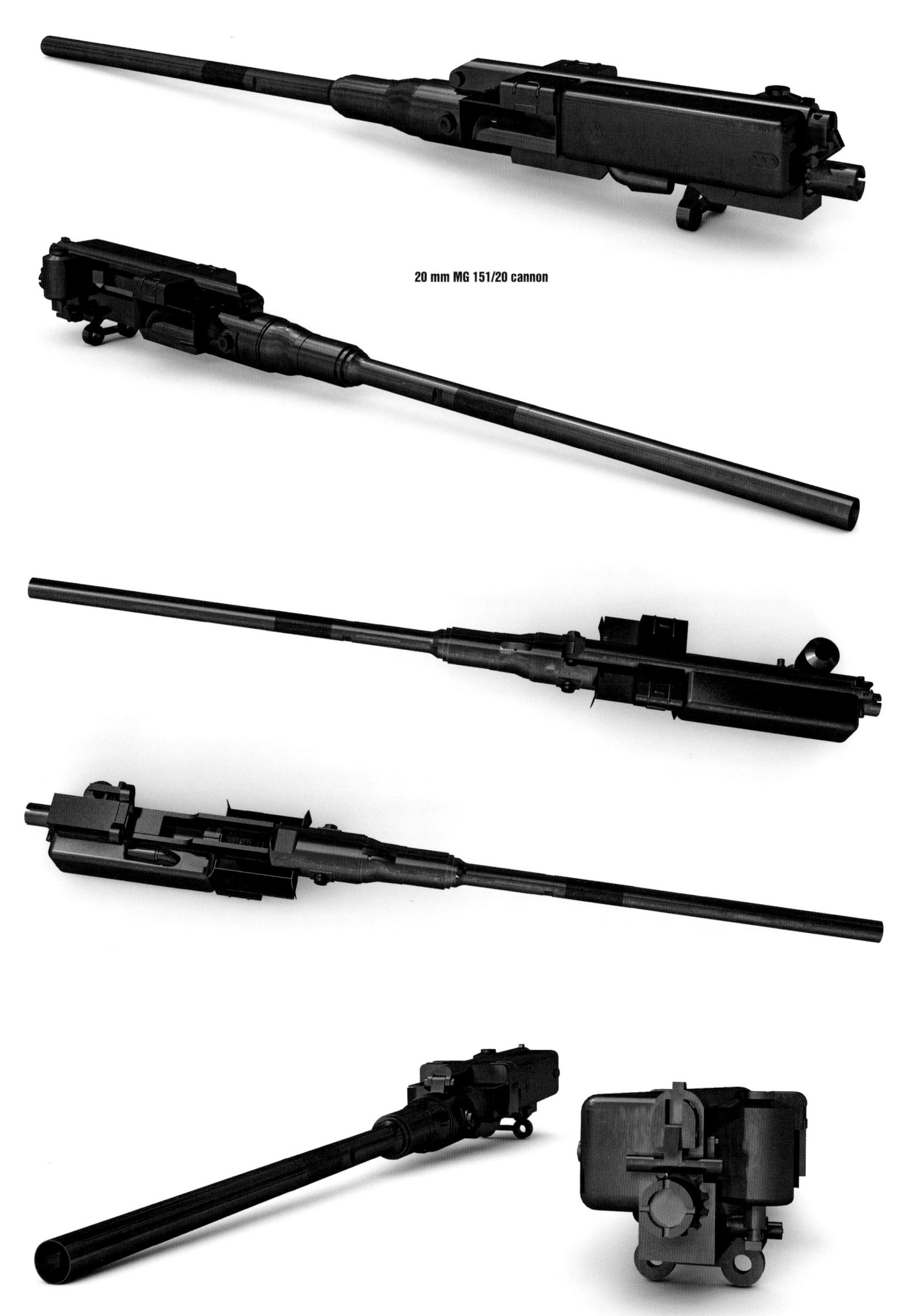

3D rendering by Stefan Dramiński

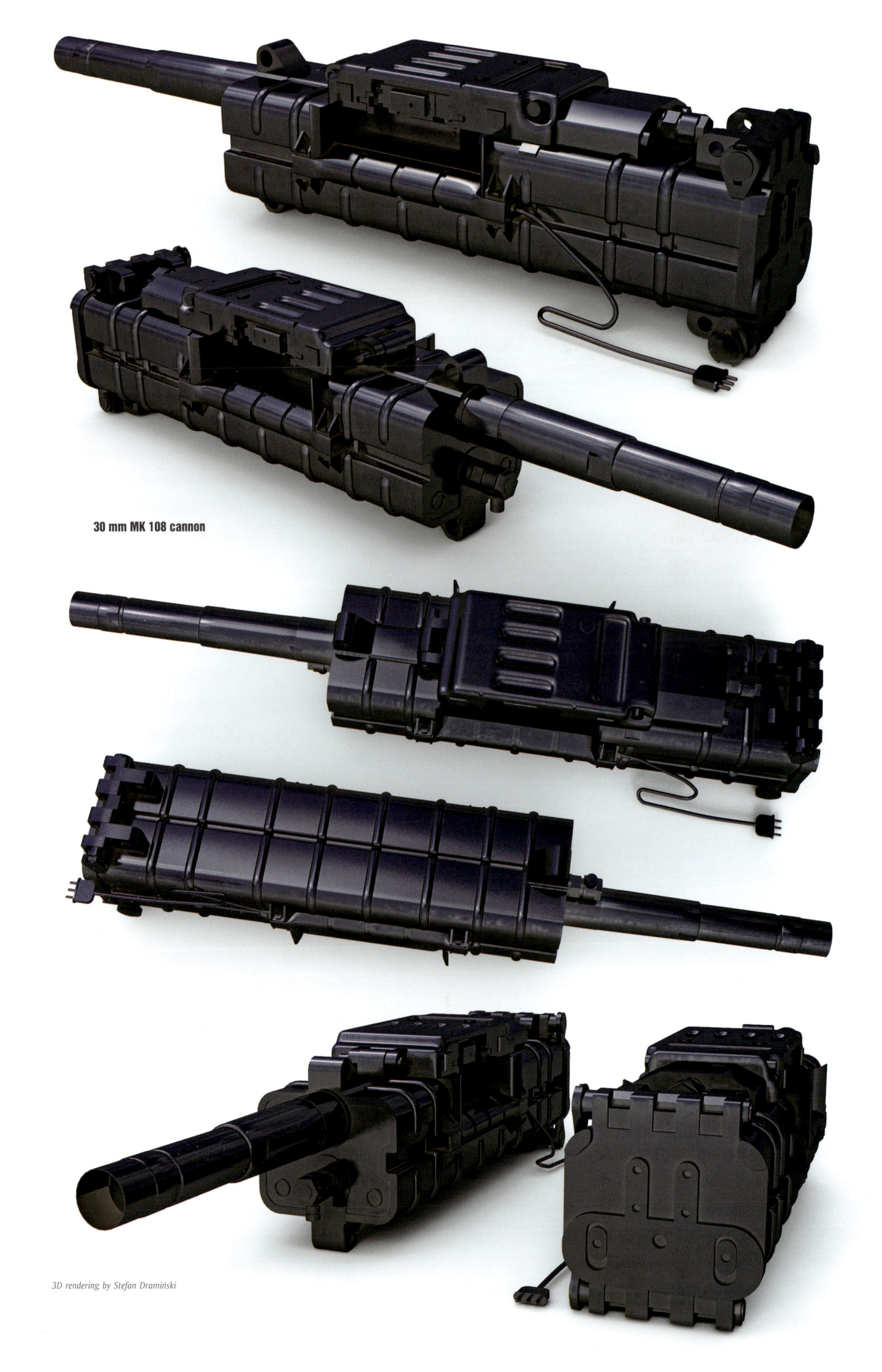

30 mm MK 108 cannon

3D rendering by Stefan Dramiński

Revi 16B gunsight

3D rendering by Stefan Dramiński

Painted by Arkadiusz Wróbel

Tank Ta 152 H-0, W.Nr. 150 010, „Green 4", Stab/JG 301, pilot Ofw. Walter Loos, Neustadt-Glewe airfield, 30 April 1945. The aircraft sports the RLM 82/83/76 paint scheme with yellow and red stripe of the Defence of the Reich, the tactical number is green with black outline, the spinner is painted RLM 70 with a white spiral.

Tank Ta 152 H-0, „Yellow 1" of 7./JG 301, this aircraft was flown among others by Ofw. Willi Reschke, Alteno airfield, April 1945. The aircraft sports the RLM 82/83/76 paint scheme with yellow and red stripe of the Defence of the Reich around the aft fuselage, the tactical number is yellow with black outline, a horizontal yellow bar with black outline – the symbol of III. Gruppe is painted on the stripe, the upper part of the cross on the fuselage is partially painted over, the spinner is painted RLM 70.

Painted by Arkadiusz Wróbel

Upper view of the Tank Ta 152 H-0, "Yellow 1" of 7./JG 301, in RLM 82/83/76 paint scheme with yellow and red stripe of the Defence of the Reich around the aft fuselage and the spinner painted RLM 70.

Painted by Arkadiusz Wróbel

Tank Ta 152 H-0, W.Nr. 150 010, CW+CJ, Newark Army Air Base, September 1945. The aircraft sports the RLM 82/83/76 paint scheme with the spinner painted RLM 70 with a white spiral. Painted over letters of the Stammkennzeichen are visible on fuselage sides.

Tank Ta 152 V30/U1, W.Nr. 0055, GH+KT, Adelheide airfield, 6 August 1944. The aircraft sports RLM 82/83/76 paint scheme.

Painted by Arkadiusz Wróbel

Tank Ta 152 H-0, W.Nr. 150 168, „Green 9", Stab/JG 301, pilot Ofw. Willi Reschke, Neustadt-Glewe airfield, 24 April 1945. The aircraft sports the RLM 82/83/76 paint scheme with yellow and red stripe of the Defence of the Reich, the tactical number is green with black outline, the spinner is painted RLM 70 with a white spiral.

Tank Ta 152 V5, W.Nr. 150 005, CW+CE, Cottbus, December 1944. The aircraft sports RLM 82/83/76 paint scheme with the spinner painted RLM 70.

First source of information
www.kagero